UNCOMMON II
Black Can Make a Difference

MEL KING

Copyright © 2023 by Mel King

All rights reserved. This book or any portion thereof may not be reproduced or transmitted in any form or manner, electronic or mechanical, including photocopying, recording, or by any information storage or retrieval system, without the express written permission of the copyright owner except for the use of brief quotations in a book review or other noncommercial uses permitted by copyright law.

Printed in the United States of America
Library of Congress Control Number: 2022923015
ISBN: Softcover   979-8-88622-851-9
        e-Book   979-8-88622-852-6
Republished by: PageTurner Press and Media LLC
Publication Date: 01/03/2023

To order copies of this book, contact:
PageTurner Press and Media
Phone: 1-888-447-9651
info@pageturner.us
www.pageturner.us

A New Beginning

I was heading west into an unknown future. The year, 1970, the month of September. Just a few days ago I was discharged from the Air Force at McGuire, AFB in New Jersey. From there I drove to Indianapolis to see my older brother, Bruce, for a couple of days. While with my brother, we had a chance to talk and I shared with him some of my experiences.

Well Mel, if you had to do it all over again, would you do it?" Bruce asked.

Without hesitation, "Yes, I would do it again." I replied.

"What would you change or do differently?"

"I think one on my biggest decisions that I had to make was leaving the Air Force Academy. Unfortunately, I won't know if that was a good decision or bad decision until later in life. Right now, I still believe it was the right choice, for me. I had a couple of friends there, who were with me at the Academy Prep School, who wanted to quit because I was leaving. I convinced them to stay. I told them 'You can't live your life through me or anyone else. My circumstances are different from yours. I am a couple of years older, I have been in the service, I will go back to the service. When I ger out, I will have the G.I. Bill to help me through college and the VA to help me buy a home. You quit now, you won't have either of those. Stay here and get an education, a degree, then after that, make your decision.'"

"You really thought this through, didn't you?"

"When my decision was made known, which was almost immediately, I was bombarded daily by my peers and a lot of upper classmen. I had to defend my position and decision constantly, so I had a lot of opportunity to 2nd guess myself."

"I notice you have some artwork with you. Keeping it in the family huh?"

"Yeah, I tried to capture what I was feeling and experiencing at various times and location."

"Mind showing me a couple and tell me what motivated you?"

"Sure. I'll try to put them in order as I experienced them."

"This first drawing is a young lady that I met in Los Angeles who was visiting some relatives in Los Angeles. I drew this picture while I was at Seymour Johnson AFB, in North Carolina. I was 18 at the time. When I left the Academy, I went to Chicago to see her. I rented a hotel not far from where she lived, in which I was going to stay, but I don't think her mom liked that idea. So, her mom had a spare bedroom that she insisted that I stay in. Smart mom."

"How long were you in Chicago?"

"Just for about four days. When I left there, I was heading to Los Angeles for about two weeks. But let's get back to the time-line.

As I was leaving Seymour Johnson, you can see the influence that the service can have on a young, gullible, and inexperienced youngster. I had just turned 19, and had gotten orders to go to Thailand. The Lady in the middle reminded me of a friend and is why she is the dominant picture. As far as the lady with. . . you name the expression. Well, I saw the pain, and agony of the soul of many Black woman here in the South and I wanted to capture that. Many of them felt like there was no hope, but if they got connected with a service guy, seriously connected, they believed it was their ticket out. It worked for many; however, and unfortunately it also didn't work for many. The service guys took advantage of this situation, which I believe only added to the frustration of the Black women there. There was a lady friend that I met in Goldsboro, the town right outside of Seymour Johnson, that I had known. But she had a relative in Washington D.C., and she was asked to come live with her relative. I drove her up to D.C. and we said our good byes, knowing that we would never see each other again."

"That must have been hard on you?"

"Yeah, that one was. She was smart and a beautiful young lady. This other picture I did when I was in Thailand. We were at war in Vietnam and against Vietnam. Problem was, some of the other folks in the area didn't get the same message. We had Pathot Loa, guys that were sympathetic to the Vietnam cause, constantly firing at us or trying to infiltrate the base. And here I am stationed in Thailand, working the same hours and days, and getting shot at, as my counterpart is in Vietnam; yet, they get combat pay and we didn't. Politicians need to come out and get in our foxholes sometime. Anyhow the hand and eye is the 'Uncle Sam Wants You', and the rifle, bayonet, and hand-grenade are all symbols of our weaponry and what we could expect when we answer the call to duty. But you know brother, as they say, 'There are no atheist in fox holes.' That is so true. Tell me what else do you see, especially in the smoke coming from the rifle barrel."

"Well, I didn't think much of it, but I'll look. OK, I see it. It looks like a cross."

"Yeah. There were a couple of times when I wished I had a fox hole to crawl into. I tell you what, those kinds of experiences can give you a whole new perspective on life. . . and death."

"It looks like you made it through OK."

"I did, but there were a couple of times when it could have been very different."

"This last drawing is about my leaving the service. I did this one at Maguire, AFB in New Jersey.

The young lady is Frances. We have been dating and seeing each other since High School."

"She's a looker."

"Yeah, she gets a lot of attention. She is an airline stewardess for Western Airlines. I hope to be able to renew our friendship. My discharge date was September 15h, hence the calendar, and it so happens that my birthday is in September, which means that I am a Libra, therefore the scales."

"What's the booze for? I know you don't drink hard liquor."

"That, I think I just wanted the challenge of drawing the bottle." We both laughed.

"Mel, you draw really good, the detail is amazing. Have you had any training?"

"No, just art classes in high school, along with everyone else. Bruce, you should know, art runs in the family."

I stayed with Bruce for about two and a half days, and from there, on to Denver. After spending a couple of days in Denver, visiting Rick and his family, and Dee, I got on the road again. I met Rick while at the Air Force Academy. He was an instructor. As mentioned in my prior Memoir, my military background and South-East Asia (SEA) experience permitted me to gain quick recognition and acceptance by those that were in the military. Rick, was no exception. I became a friend and not just as a cadet. When I left the Academy, we stayed in touch and I promised that I would stop in Denver to see him on my way home when I got out of the service. So now I am driving through the Rocky Mountains in a used car, which I purchased for $300, that won't go any faster than 55 mph without a "Whole lot of Shakin' going on." I had an abundance of time to think over the past few months of my service life and to think of my future. What is waiting for me in L.A.? I didn't have a job lined up. My sister, Vic, and her husband, George, were gracious enough to let me stay with them for, "No more than six months," I said. Oh well, I can only take a day at a time.

First Job

After being in LA for about a week, I landed a job in a mailroom for Aero Jet General (AJ). This opportunity came about through a young lady, Frances, whom I had been dating since high school. Frances had a family friend that worked in Human Resources at Aero Jet and she was able to persuade him to let me fill the job after the first interview. The company had difficulty keeping people in the mailroom. Those that did work in the mailroom often times didn't show up on time for work, had frequent absenteeism, or they needed an attitude adjustment. Me, I was at work everyday, on time, and I walked through the facility saying "Hi" to people on my route. Although I did my job

Victoria & George

and I did it as best I could, I couldn't help thinking about General Olds and the picture he painted when I submitted my resignation from the Air Force Academy. Because of my leadership skills that I had exhibited, he told me how much I would be appreciated in the military, contrasting that to civilian life. I thought about the responsibility at McGuire, AFB. Heading up a group, of at least a dozen people, with complete authority and responsibility of a major program on the base; Stripping, cleaning and repainting the giant C-141 multimillion-dollar cargo aircrafts. Here, as a civilian, no personnel responsibility, no project oversight, no senior officers commenting on a job well done, here, I am just pushing a cart delivering mail.

Although this was the first time, I thought about General Olds comment since I left the Academy; "Civilians don't often appreciate nor reward leadership, innovation, or dedication. The service does and has recognized innate leadership in you; which, will not necessarily be so in the civilian sector where politics and envy can come into play," it wasn't the last.

Now would probably be a good time to tell you a little about Frances. Red, Gregory, and I (my buddies from Junior and Senior High School) were doing our thing at a party; that is, getting it started. We were in our sophomore year in High School. Many times, we would get to a party and the girls would be on one side of the room talking and the guys would be on the other side. It reminded me of "Animal Planet" where no one Wildebeest wanted to be the first to cross a crocodile infested river. Red, Gregory, and I had a set routine to get a party going. First, we would scope out the room, determine which of the girls we plan to dance with, make any lighting adjustments (dim, but not dark), and finally select the proper slow record to play. This one time the party was being hosted by one of the girls we met previously that went to an all-girls Catholic school called Bishop Conaty.

Me, I saw this one young lady that had jet black hair, hair that was cut kind of in a shag, light caramel skin, and had a terrific smile. She was fairly animated and seemed friendly enough in talking with her girl-friends, but I didn't know if that would carry over to a guy she never met before. What the heck. Red got the lights, Gregory worked out the music, and I cleared everything with the host. The party was about to get on. As the lights dimmed, and a slow song played, everyone stopped talking. It was obvious something different was about to happen. Red, Greg and I, came back together and as one, started toward our pre-selected targets. All the girls, and even the guys, turned to look at us. In some ways, it did feel like we were crossing a crocodile infested river, but cross we did. We didn't know how the girls would respond, but we took the chance that they were here to dance so we were going to give them that opportunity. As I approached the girls, this one young lady initially had her back to us, but began turning around when the lights were dimmed and the music began playing. As she turned around, I noticed her slim but shapely figure, the curiosity in her eyes, and her straight and upright frame. Everything that I could tell about her, outwardly, indicated that she was a very confident person, one that wouldn't hesitate to decline a dance request. As I approached, and she began to realize that I was approaching her, a slight smile began to show on her face. I didn't know if it was a "Watch this, girls, how I will humiliate this guy, or a hmm, glad to know you're interested smile." Fortunately, it was the latter, and the party was on as both guys and girls began to intermingle. The young lady's name was Frances and we began seeing one another quite often after that initial meeting and ultimately, I took Francis to my senior prom.

After high school, Frances took a job as a stewardess with Western Airlines. One evening, shortly after being out of the service, we were going to Hollywood to visit the Magic Castle.

While going she said "Take La Brea Avenue instead of Highland Avenue. I want to show you something."

Highland Ave. would have been faster to where we were going, but we had plenty of time, even in the L.A. traffic. We were doing the small talk when I stopped mid-stream, pulled the car over, stopped, got out of the car and just stared. Looking back at me on a billboard was a giant-sized half-body picture of Frances in her Western Airlines outfit. The company had selected her to be the face of Western Airlines. Wow!

The conversation was fairly animated as we discussed her selection to promote her company while we continued on to the Magic Castle. The Magic Castle is a "Members Only" club, although I was not a member. A few months earlier I had gone to the Castle with a friend and met the "Senator," the proprietor. He took a liking to me and said if I ever wanted to come to the Castle, just give him a call. So here we were, riding to Hollywood to go to the Castle. We did the Valet parking and went to guest reservations.

"Hi, I'm here to see the Senator" I said.

The receptionist looked at me with obvious dis-belief.

"And who shall I say wants to see him?" As she stared me down.

"Mel, Mel King"

"Just a minute, I'll see if I can locate him."

She makes a couple of calls, then we heard,

"Senator, you have a gentleman by the name of Mel King asking for you. [Pause] You know him sir? [Pause] Yes, I'll let the attendant know. [Pause] Yes Sir."

She hangs up the phone.

And with apparent unbelief still on her face, says, "The Senator said that you may come in, for me to have someone show you where the Dining Room is, and that he will come and say 'Hi,' to you shortly." Her face continued to register unbelief.

During the dinner, the Senator did come by

to talk with us and gave us a personal invite to attend his Midnight performance. We didn't know it at the time, but to be invited to any performance given by the Senator was a rare treat. After dinner, we went to a couple of performances conducted by other magicians, until it was time to go see the Senator. We went to the venue where the Senator was performing. We approached the entrance and saw the attendants standing there checking invitations. Oh, oh, we didn't have an invitation. In my mind, I was wondering what can I say to get us in. A lot of things went through my mind, but eventually it settled on the truth, "The Senator invited us." I was preparing to go into my spiel when one of the attendants looked up and saw us.

"You must be Mel and the lovely lady must be Frances?" said the attendant.

"Well, uh, yes I am and yes she is," I said. (Didn't see any other Black faces the whole night so he stood a good chance of being correct.}

"Good, come with me."

The attendant escorted us to our "front row" seats.

"Enjoy the show." The attendant said as he walked back up the aisle.

The Senator had saved two seats down front for us. It probably didn't hurt that Frances was wearing short-shorts at the time. It wasn't long before the Senator came on stage.

"What magician is a good magician, unless he has some beautiful young lady to assist him with his magic?" said the Senator, first thing, as he looks out over the audience.

The room held about 75 people. The small seating also helped to make this a prized viewing.

The Senator continued to scan the audience, from the back to the front. As his eyes panned the front row he settled upon Frances.

"Ah, Frances, why don't you come up and join me on stage?"

"Me?" said Frances.

"Of course, my dear. Please, come join me."

Reluctantly, Frances went up on stage. In her short-shorts she looked the part. The Senator gave a great performance and was a great culmination to a great evening.

We continued to date a few years after that until she moved out of town.

The job situation at AJ that I found myself in was not necessarily without intent. Prior to leaving the service I sent in an application to the L.A. Post Office. When I got to L.A., I received a letter asking me to come down to take a test. Only a few days had past before I received word to come back to the Postal office for an interview. Although the Post Office had about a six-month waiting list of candidates, I was given priority over the other candidates because I was a Vietnam Vet. It didn't hurt that I had scored well on the test. During the interview, the interviewer said that he received authorization to make a job offer to me that very day. Needless to say, I was very excited. The Post Office paid very well, had great benefits, and, if I chose, long term security. As quickly as my elation came, it just as quickly vanished.

I asked the interviewer, "What are the hours?"

"Since you will be the junior person where-ever we send you, your schedule will vary. It may be day shift, swing shift, or graveyard. I don't know," he said.

At that I said, "Then I cannot accept the job."

"What!" The interviewer exclaimed. "We have a six-month waiting list of people clamoring to get into the Post Office, you have a job offered to you, and you turn it down?"

"You see sir; I have a goal. When I was in high school, I set a goal for myself to have my Master's degree within 12 years of graduation. If I accept this job, I will not be able to go to night school and begin my education. The goal that I set for myself will be delayed; and possibly, with the money and security of the Post Office, I may lose my incentive to even go to school. I can't afford to take the risk of being sidetracked from my goal."

The interviewer sat back in his chair, looked at me with studied eyes and said, "I marvel at your determination and commitment. It is more the reason why we need people like you in the Post Office. Never-the-less, I understand. Let me wish you well."

Shortly after the interview with the Post Office, I was called to an interview with a drug store chain. I went on the interview. During the interview, the interviewer said that because I was a Vietnam Vet, and if the interview went well, he had authorization to make a job offer to me that very day. Needless to say, I was very excited. The position was a Management Trainee position. The drug store paid very well, had great benefits, and, if I chose, long term security. As quickly as my elation came, it just as quickly vanished.

I asked the interviewer, "What are the hours?"

"Since you will be in training, your schedule will vary. It may be day shift, swing shift, or a little bit of both during the same week. I don't know," he said.

At that I said, "Then I cannot accept the job."

"What!" The interviewer exclaimed. "We have a long waiting list of people clamoring to just get an interview, you have a job offered to you, and you turn it down?"

"You see sir; I have a goal. When I was in high school, I set a goal for myself to have my Master's degree within 12 years of graduation. If I accept this job, I will not be able to go to night school and begin my education. The goal that I set for myself will be delayed; and possibly, with the money and security that this company offers, I may lose my incentive to go to school. I can't afford to take the risk of being sidetracked from my goal."

The interviewer sat back in his chair, looked at me with studied eyes and said, "I marvel at your determination and commitment. It is more the reason why we need people like you in this company. Never-the-less, I understand. Let me wish you well."

With that, my fate was sealed. I turned down two exceptional job offers due to their potential distraction from my goal. With that, I was committed to finding a job that would permit me to go to night school. Hence, I find myself walking through the halls of Aero Jet General delivering mail, at a much lower salary than what was offered at the Post Office and drug store.

It didn't take long before my diligence at AJ began to pay off. Along with my mail-room duties, I was asked to provide oversight to the fleet of about 15 vehicles owned by the company. I was responsible for their maintenance and upkeep during my employment with AJ. Many of the Vice-presidents knew me and would often ask if I would have their personal vehicle serviced while at work. By now I had several repair shops that I was confident in and whom I felt were reasonable in their fees. I am not sure why, but sometimes when we had out of town managers come in, and a group was going to lunch, oftentimes I would be invited to go along. On one such occasion I was away from the plant at a repair shop so I told the coordinating manager that I would meet them at the restaurant. I got to the restaurant early so I parked in a spot just to the side and slightly behind the restaurant. As I was sitting there, one of the workers pulled up and began unloading her vehicle. She had a lot of stuff.

I got out of the car and said to her, "Do you need some help? I'm just waiting for some guys to show up. We're having lunch here, so I have plenty of time."

"That would be great. Thank you," she said.

I made a couple of trips as I helped her carry her things into the restaurant. It didn't hurt that she was a rather attractive lady. She was overly thankful, as she said that she was running late and had to hurry.

"No problem, as I said, I was just waiting for some guys to show up."

"Good. I will see you inside then?"

"Uh, I guess so. Depends on what you do."

"I'll look for you," she said..

"It's a deal," I said as she was hurrying inside. Doesn't hurt to have an attractive young lady come looking for you, I thought.

The guys arrive and we go inside for lunch. I took a quick look around and didn't see my lady friend. We sat at two, four-person booths with me sitting on the inside of one of the booths. We ordered lunch and it was during lunch that I saw the lady that I had help unload her car. Chalk it up to my naiveté but I had no clue as to the type of place we were having lunch. There she was, my lady friend, center stage, doing a poll dance number, beginning to undress. I looked around at the guys, they were giving her their rapt attention. Me, I felt very uncomfortable. One of the guys at our table whistled. It got her attention. She looked at him and kinda smiled. But now that she was looking in our direction, she spotted me, pointed, and blew me a kiss. All the guys, in unison, turned their heads and looked at me. No place to run, no place to hide. In my embarrassment, I'm sure I lit up the place as dim as it was. My lady friend didn't help. When she saw that the guys immediately began to heckle me, she added fuel to the fire. She would purposely strike a pose or make an evocative move in my direction that sent, not only the guys crazy, but now the whole restaurant was picking up on what was happening. The crowd was loving it. People started throwing money at her, every time she made a gesture in my direction. She obviously became motivated. I was embarrassed beyond embarrassment. Lunch couldn't get over fast enough. I put my head down on the table, ostrich style, thinking if I didn't see, I couldn't be seen. This gal was good. Somehow, she managed to turn the guys I'm sitting with into her stage-hands. They were at her beck and call. When she made notice that she was coming in our direction, the guys would cause me to raise my head; and, when she went elsewhere, they would lower my head again. This was repeated several times until she worked the crowd into a frenzy. I thought, this is what I get for being a gentleman. Oh well.

"Wow, Mel am I glad we invited you along. I have been here a couple of times before, but never was it this much fun." The manager said.

"Yeah, next time you get to help carry her bags in," I said.

Following his comment, I thought, 'it was probably the most entertaining lunch that many people had in a long time.'

I spent almost two years with Aero Jet General.

East Los Angeles College

While working at Aero Jet, which was located in El Monte, California, just east of Los Angeles, I started going to night school at East Los Angeles Junior College. I would leave work and go directly to school where I would continue my studying and whatever other homework assignment I had. I was taking 12 units (equivalent to a fulltime load), going to school Monday through Thursday, from 7:00 PM to 10:00 PM each semester until I graduated with an Associate of Arts degree in June of 1973. Each semester I took a math course, starting with Algebra II and ending with Calculus II. I even had a couple of courses on reading a slide rule. The course I really enjoyed though was my engineering design class. As in high school, the instructor appreciated my work and often had it displayed. While at East LA, I made an "A" in all my classes except for one course in my last semester. I got a "B" in Calculus II.

I made some really good friends while at East LA. One, whom I'll call Larry, became a really close friend and often would spend our study time together. Since I was single, he and his wife would occasionally invite me over for dinner. For you married couples, that have a few single friends, let me tell you, a home cooked meal is…wonderful. Remember that. Unfortunately, Larry, shortly after I met him, went through a divorce. Me, working full-time and going to night school full-time didn't leave much room for anything else, …well… maybe for a few extra curricular activities. I had a set schedule. Work and school during the week. Friday was hallelujah night. Not that I went to church or anything, I was just grateful to have the night off and I took full advantage of the time. Saturday and Sunday were study time. No interference, none whatsoever. If a party came up on Saturday, I would swap out Friday as study night. My friends accepted my regimen and tried to work with me. As I got home from work, on Fridays, I would make calls to my friends to follow up on prior arrangements. Once the destination and possible association (as in female acquaintance) was determined, I got in a little study just to lighten the load on Saturday. At 9:00 PM I'm walking out the door to, as they say in the hood, "PARTAE." I didn't know what curfew was. And since I didn't count Saturday as study time until I got home, some Saturdays started very late.

Sunday was not only a day for study but was also my day for cooking. Because I didn't get home from school until 10:30 – 10:45 PM at night during the week, it was too late to try and cook something. To counter the late, mid-week cooking, I would cook on Sunday what I was going to eat for the rest of the week. I would determine what I was going to eat, and then call my sister, Vic, and get my weekly cooking lesson.

Sometimes I would get TV dinners as an option and as a change. Besides, I initially needed the TV dinners, not so much for the dinners themselves, but for the tray. Microwave ovens didn't exist at the time, so I needed some kind of container to heat food that would go into a conventional oven. Empty TV dinner trays worked great. When I prepared the meals on Sunday, I would pull out old TV dinner trays that had been cleaned and put away, just for this occasion. I would take what I cooked and put them in the tray, wrap it really good in aluminum foil and stick them in the freezer. My brother Paul would come to visit sometimes and there were a few occasions where I pulled out my home prepared TV dinners.

One day he commented, "I need to know where you go to get your TV dinners, they're much better than the one's I get."

Jokingly I said, "Son, you are eating a home cooked meal, prepared by yours truly."

"No, way!"

"Yep. Do it every Sunday."

Paul looked at his plate, "Incredible."

Since I would go to school directly from work, often times I was the first to arrive at school. As is often the case with most students, I/ we had our own special table or location in which we sat. Over time, there got to be eight to ten of us sitting together, guys and gals, Black, Hispanic, Caucasian, and well, anyone and everyone was welcomed. We even had a foreign exchange student from Germany join us. There was no such thing as "Political Correctness" at the time so anything and everything was discussed. It also was a time when guys like the gals and the gals liked us guys. There was no thought of it being any different. Mondays were usually pretty lively as everyone talked about their weekend. Some of the stories were fairly graphic, and surprisingly, the ladies in the group were the most descriptive. We had a few individuals that came and went, but they were often pulled in by the core group as a date or a person of interest. We got to know each other so well that on one occasion, we had an open discussion about a person of interest that was sitting with us, and that person had no clue that we were talking about them.

As the first year progressed, Larry and I talked about going skiing in the local area mountains. The rest of the group didn't show any interest in going, but always joined in to talk about the many ways we would break a leg, ankle or other members of our body. None of us had any experience in skiing, so it was going to be quite a venture. Snow Valley was a place that we "heard about." Being Black and not knowing anyone else that skied made information gathering about skiing a little difficult (The internet didn't' exist). It didn't help that we were in a Latino area; Latinos were not prone to skiing either. Boy, were we in the dark ages. Thing was, we didn't know we were in the dark ages. What a difference the internet has made. We "talked" about going skiing the whole months of December, January, February, and March. The weekends would come and go, and every week we would say, "Let's go skiing in two weeks." Two weeks would come and go; and it was always the next two weeks. We missed that first year of skiing. The following year, once again Larry and I made a promise to go skiing. Once again December and January came and went. During the last week of January in 1972, the group was together laughing and talking, when someone jokingly said,

"Hey Mel, Larry, are you guys going skiing like last year?"

We responded, "Yea, we're going to qualify for the Olympics."

We all laughed. However, Larry and I looked at each other, a slight nod, this weekend would be the weekend we did it.

First Time Skiing - Snow Valley

Saturday morning, we got up bright and early. We were on the road by 6:00 AM. It was an hour and 45-minute drive to Snow Valley (see Figure 4 – 1), the ski area that we decided to bless with our presence. Snow Valley is located in the San Bernardino Mountain range, about 90 miles east of L.A. The drive is mostly Freeway, except when you get to the foothills. From the foothills, there is a two-lane highway going up the mountain with several passing lanes as you progress. As we pulled into the parking lot, we had no clue what to do. So, we started asking people that were dressed liked they knew what they were doing. Some, after we talked to them just looked at us with this knowing smile, and as they were turning away said "Break a leg." I thought 'Break a Leg, I'll break your leg.' The first time this happened, Larry and I looked at each other, did a quick evaluation and figured we were way outnumbered to start a ruckus. Didn't see another black face nowhere around, not even close. We wanted to jump the guy. By the third time this happened, we realized that it was the skier's way of conveying "Good Luck." Boy, did we have a lot to learn. And that was just the beginning. We saw a couple that seemed to have friendly faces and asked them about lift tickets. We saw a line, thought it was for tickets, but wanted to make sure.

"Where do we go to buy tickets? Do the skis and stuff come with the tickets?" We asked.

"Well, have you skied before?"

"Nope. First time up."

"Well, you should get the combo package that includes lift ticket, skis, boots, and poles. Join the line over there and just ask at the ticket booth."

"Thanks."

We walked to the ticket booth.

"How much is a beginner's lift ticket, with skis, boots and poles?

With a slight chuckle, "We don't have beginner's lift tickets. We just have prices for youngsters, students and adults. Which are you?" The ticket agent asked.

"Oh. Both of us are students. How much is a student lift ticket with skis boots and poles?

"Do you want the regular or deluxe package? The regular package is $10.00 the Deluxe package is $11.00. I assume you are beginners; therefore, I would recommend the regular package."

We bought our tickets and went to the ski rental shop to get our equipment.

"Well, hi boys, what can we do for you today?"

In my mind I thought, "Boy", who are you calling boy?" But once again I remembered where we were, fully outnumbered.'

"We're here to get outfitted with all this stuff. We were told to come here," I said.

"Well, you came to the right spot. I'll fix you right up. First time skiing, huh? (must have been really obvious) Well, we'll take care of you."

"Yep. First time. Been saying all last year we were going to go but never did."

"OK. Once I make the adjustment then I'll show you how to get in and out of your ski."

The outfitters ended up being nice guys. They got us fitted out, showed us how to get in and out of our ski and sent us on our way.

One thing about skiing, in which we were oblivious, there is this code of conduct that must be adhered to. Skiers for the most part are very polite.

When coming down the mountain, you yell out, "On your right," or "On your left."

If someone falls, you help to retrieve skis, glove, goggles or poles. If you run over someone's skis, you apologize. If you bump into them while in line, you apologize, etc. Because we didn't know, I think we violated most of the codes that day. Anyhow we emerged from the shadow of the lodge into a bright, sun-shiny day. We had on blue jeans and some kind of coat. I won't say "parka," that would be too generous. Without even asking, the other skiers would look at us and know we were beginners. One thing for sure, Larry and I knew we were going to like skiing. The ladies in these ski outfits, Oh yeah! We figured all we had to do was ski a few runs, get reasonably good, and then we could talk stuff in the lodge. We couldn't wait until this day was over. After all, we both were good athletes and skiing couldn't be all that tough.

Before we left, one of the guys at the fitting room showed us how to use our pole straps to carry our skis. We followed his instructions, got our skis together, and asked for directions to the beginner or "Bunny Slope" as they are called. We were ready to conquer this mountain. Just in case you were thinking it, no, the thought of getting skiing lessons never entered our minds. We put on our boots, gathered our skis and poles and started out. Because of the boots, due to their stiffness and since we had laced them all the way, we began walking like Frankenstein. We got close to the chairlift for the Bunny Slope, put on our skis… and fell. That was not suppose to happen. After all, we were macho athletes. We stood up again and fell again.

Another beginner came by and said, "You need to stand up parallel to the hill."

Hill, what hill. About now it looked very much like a mountain. However, we took his advice, made our skis parallel to the hill, stood up… and fell.

Another beginner came by and said, "The skis need to be parallel to the hill, but downhill."

Since we were already on our backs, we just rolled over and brought our skis from the uphill side of the mountain to where they were parallel, but downhill from us. Larry and I exchanged looks, once again with that instant understanding, this was going to be our triumphant attempt. We stood up and…we continued to stand. Yeah! Victory! Once we were up, we were able to gain a little balance. We slowly, very slowly, inched our way toward the chairlift. We never gave thought about how we were going to get off that darn thing. Right now, our job was to get to it. Just as we got close to the line, the hill took a little drop. It was just enough to get us going beyond our control. We had no clue how to stop on these things. I didn't know what to say except the one word that I have heard being cried out when you want someone to look out,

"Fore." I called out.

OK, so that's in golf, still, it worked. People turned around saw that we were out of control and burst out laughing, except for those in our path. The hill was not very steep, we were not going very fast, but still, to us, it seemed like we were run-away freight trains. A couple of guys who were not beginners tried to grab us and keep us from plowing into everybody and creating a "domino effect." Too late. I'm sure, for any observer of this event, they were fully entertained as they saw a slow wave begin to develop as one skier after another began to lose their balance and fall. As the wave snaked through the line, claiming one skier after another, it finally hit a wall. Fortunately, there were of couple of guys in line that were not beginners and all they did was to back out of the way and let the last domino fall. Why these guys were in line, I don't know, but certainly glad they were. They began helping all of us get to our feet, stabilized us and got us pointed in the right direction. By now we were on relatively flat ground, so we felt pretty confident that we could make it to the chairlift without falling again.

From a distance, the chairlift looked like it was moving so-o-o slowly. Now that we were in line, and got closer to the lift, we wondered, "Who sped this darn thing up?" The chairlift looked to be going so fast it could launch aircraft from a carrier deck. Fast or slow, we came this far, we weren't going to back down now. As I said, we were the only "people of color" on the whole mountain (I would guess that there was about 4500 people on the mountain, and about 40 in line at the chairlift), so we knew a bunch of eyes were on us. As we approached the lift, we had a mix of dread and exhilaration. We were finally going to do it, go skiing. We moved forward to the loading area. We were shuffling and waving our poles about, trying to keep our balance for the last couple of feet until we were rescued by the chairlift. Just as we were about to fall again, the chair was there, hitting us on the back of the legs and forcing us to sit down. Amazing grace. Larry and I looked at each other and began laughing. We made it on the chairlift. We were taking this thing one challenge at a time. We knew the next one would be getting off this dog-gone thing. Who sped this thing up again? Before we knew it, it was time to prepare to get off. We had no clue of what to do. To this day, we don't know who caused who to fall. We barely got out of the chair when, wham, we fell and fell hard. Actually, it was almost as if it was in slow motion. The sun got brighter, I heard things more clearly, and I saw the ground coming at me as if it was on a mission. Of course, we caused the attendant to stop the chair.

We crawled our way out of the path, or runway as it is called, dusted the snow off of each other, regained our composure, and laughed again. When we inched our way around to see downhill, no, down the mountain, it looked impossible that anyone could navigate that steep slope. Yet, there were other beginners coming off the chair and heading downhill without hesitation. We stood there a while to observe the various techniques before settling on a "V" formation. We later learned that this was called a snowplow or wedge position. We were parallel to the mountain, so we knew we weren't going anywhere. The question was how do you transition from being parallel to begin heading downhill and staying upright? "Upright" was the operative word. Well, we figured the polls we had in our hands were there for a reason, and that was to push. We pushed ourselves around and started downhill. For the next few moments, we alternated between exhilaration and stark fear. It must have been obvious that we were very, very, new beginners, cause even the other beginners gave us a wide berth and didn't come near. The run was about 200 yards. It felt like we fell two hundred times. However, every time we got up, we counted it all joy.

We eventually made it back to the chairlift line, without wiping out half the people. We got on the chair without incident and focused on getting off the chair without falling. On the one run we made, we actually began to get the feel of the skis and the balance needed to stay upright. So, by the time we got back on the chairlift, we began to think about what and how we would get off the chairlift. Over and over, we spoke out loud what we were going to do; and, practiced in the chair, poles in the outer hand, lean forward, plant skis on the snow, stand up. Poles in the outer hand, lean forward, plant skis on the snow, stand up. The moment came, poles in the outer hand, lean forward, plant skis on the snow, stand up. Victory! From that moment on, our learning began to accelerate. We made run after run, getting better each time. We made such drastic improvement, that people, who didn't see our first attempt to get on the chairlift, began asking us how many times we had gone skiing. They were amazed that this was our first day.

After our short 30-minute lunch break, I looked over at Larry, he looked at me; and without saying a word we abandoned the beginner's chairlift and headed over to the intermediate chair. If you recall, I had said earlier, that at first, the beginner's chairlift looked like it could launch a fighter from a carrier deck. If we had gone to this intermediate chair first, we would have thought it was the Space Shuttle. It was faster and the incline looked like it was pointing skyward. I thought, "Are we ready for this?" I didn't dare look at Larry. He didn't look at me. I figured at this point it would not have taken much for either of us to change our minds, so I didn't want to give it place. Without saying a word to each other, we got in line, waited for the chair, got on without a problem and then looked up. All we could see was sky. On the beginner's chair, a person could still see the mountain as a backdrop. On this chair, only time you saw the mountain is when looking down. Oh boy! By now, getting off the chair was no problem, and got off we did.

We skied, pushed our way to the "Plato," where every skier ski to looked down the mountain, say their last rights, and push off. We looked down the mountain, said our last rights, and waited, and waited, and waited. From our vantage point we were so high up we could see other peaks and valleys of the San Bernardino Mountains. Since we were already halfway to heaven, we thought that, well maybe we shouldn't rush it to make it the rest of the way. So once again we watched the other skiers to see what they were doing. We saw, what we figured was the next phase of skiing. They would start off in a snowplow stance, ski, and when they were ready to make the turn, they would bring one ski next to the other, complete the turn, and go back to the snowplow. We watched this over and over until we got a mental picture. It was now time to develop muscle memory; or in other words, time to go for it.

Off we went. Snowplow, bring ski together, plop. That is not exactly what I saw. What made matters worse was the steepness of the hill. On the Bunny slope the hill was not very steep, although it seemed like it was at the time, so when I fell, I didn't slide very far on the Bunny slope. Not so now. I slid and slid and slid. Prior to this fall, I did learn to fall on my glut, get my feet downhill and try to use the skis as a brake. Wasn't working. This was a lo-o-ong ski run. As they say in the army, "There are no atheist in fox holes." I was in a fox hole. Once I made my confession, suddenly I stopped. Wow! So, there is a God in heaven.

Didn't dwell on that subject too long, I got what I wanted. I gathered myself together, stood up, looked downhill, and started again. Snowplow, bring skis together, plop, slide. I did this over and over again until I made it down the mountain. It wasn't the most glamorous way to come down the mountain but come down I did. Moreover, and most importantly, I thought it was fun. Every time I got up, I would go a little further before I fell again. I didn't hesitate to go back to the intermediate lift. On the second run, I probably fell half the number of times than on the first run.

As the sun began setting behind another peak and the shadows got long, we knew the day was coming to a close and we would be forced off the mountain. Larry and I were one of the last ones to leave the mountain. We were trying to get in every minute we could. We finally had to go to the ski rental shop to return our skis, boots and poles, only because they stop running the chairlift. As we were walking back to the car I looked up at the mountain, felt a closeness, and accepted the challenge it seemed to give, "Are you ready for me or are you ready to quit?"

"Didn't come this far to quit, I'll see you next week." I thought.

With that thought, I sealed my/ our commitment to skiing. Remember, all last year we kept saying, we'll go skiing in two weeks. Last year, that day never came. As it turned out, after this one day, we went skiing six more weekends in a row. The only reason we didn't go more weekends was that they closed the mountain and ski season was over. It's amazing how priorities can change. Last year, we couldn't find the time to ski, this year, there wasn't enough time. We got in the car and looked back up at the mountain one last time, and began laughing, really hard. We didn't notice at first what was on the face of the mountain. But now that we were relaxed, we paid closer attention. Portions of the intermediate run we were on all day faced the main lodge and the highway. We were wearing blue jeans. What we saw, and what we believed inspired the movie, were "blue streaks." We looked down at our jeans and it looked like they had been tied dyed, especially on the right side. The right was our most favorite side in which to fall, and the jeans were bleached white in some areas.

We looked back at the mountain.

"I guess we left our mark," I said.

We laughed again. By the third time out, we were skiing the intermediate run without falling, cautiously, but not falling. On the last weekend of ski season, other skiers were amazed that this was just our first season and have skied only six times before. We were pleased with our progress. We were having so much fun we never thought about staying or sitting in the lodge. Oh well, the ladies will have to wait until next year.

A Pillar of Smoke

One night while coming home from school, around 10:30 PM, I noticed smoke coming from a detached garage, located between two houses on Arlington, near 48th St. I had passed the houses initially so I made a "U" turn in the middle of the street to go back and see if the smoke was a harbinger of something more serious. Sure 'nuff. Flames were just starting to appear in the windows of the garage. I jump out of the car, knock on the door of one of the homes.

"Hello, wake up. There is a fire in your backyard."

I finally got someone to answer the door.

"There is a fire in your backyard. Call the Fire Department. Do you have a garden hose?"

"Yes, the hose, it's around the side of the house. I'll call the Fire Department," he said.

"Good. Go get it connected and I'll let your neighbor know what's happening."

I went next door and got the neighbor's attention and had him call the Fire Department as well. Leaving the neighbor's porch, I went back to the first house to check on the garden hose. By now, the flames where on the outside of the garage and producing a lot of heat. As I was walking back toward the garage, the homeowner was silhouetted by the flames coming from the garage. If it wasn't so serious, it was a laughable sight. Him, with this little bitty garden hose, trying to put out what was now a full-blown structure fire. It was like seeing somebody peeing on a bon-fire.

I took the hose from him.

"Here, let me have that. You go make sure your wife and kids are OK."

He left to go back inside his house. To me it was obvious that we could do nothing to save the garage, so I started watering the adjacent wooden fence and bushes to keep the flames from spreading. As I turned to water the roofs, I noticed that a couple of electrical wires were already victims of the fire and were lying on the ground. We were not far from a fire station, so it wasn't very long before I heard the sound of sirens. I continued to water the fence, bushes, and rooftops, keeping them as wet as I could. As the fire trucks pulled up, the firemen began running around the trucks doing what firemen do. Finally, this lone fireman grabs a hose and runs in my direction. He comes along side of me and nods his head. I look at him and his hose. The hose was flat as there was no water coming out of it yet. Wondering why there was no water, I turned to look back at the trucks. Lo and behold. What I saw was this huge bulge in the hose signifying the front wave of the coming water. I looked at that bulge, looked at the fireman, and looked at the bulge again. No way is this fireman going to contain what was coming. My little dinky hose wasn't doing much so I abandoned it and went to join the fireman. He looked at me with appreciation.

"Thanks a lot buddy. It's going to get wild really quick." The fireman said.

That was an understatement. When that wave hit us, it was with a force that almost threw both of us on the ground. I thought, how was he planning to contain this thing by himself? No wonder he was so grateful. By now the garage was fully engulfed and would be a complete loss. I was totally surprised by the heat coming from the flames, but we stood our ground and kept the water flowing. I don't know how long we were manning the hose when a Fire Chief came into the area. By now I'm wondering where are the other firemen; and, why is it that I am still helping this fireman with the hose? The Chief doesn't come to relieve me but walks around in the backyard doing whatever Fire Chiefs do at the scene of a fire. I notice where he is walking and say,

"Chief, be careful, there is a fallen electrical line there on the ground."

"Oh yeah, I see it now. Thanks." The Chief said.

He continues his walk but away from the electrical line. By now the entire neighborhood is lining the street and sidewalk. Still, I have no relief. We continue to douse the fire with water. By now it is getting late, it has been a long day for me, and I haven't eaten dinner. I'm more than ready to go.

"I'm going to have to go, I gotta get up early and I have school tomorrow night." I tell the fireman.

"Yeah, I understand. I can dial this down a little bit. We have it under control now anyway. Really appreciate your help buddy."

"No problem. Glad I came along and stopped when I saw the smoke," I said.

"Take care buddy." The fireman said.

I left the fireman and went to get in my car. Only problem was that I was boxed in with fire trucks. I went to a fireman and asked if one of the trucks could be moved.

"Hi, would you mind moving one of your trucks so I can get out," I said.

He looked at me with an incredulous look.

"Yea, we can move it when we finish here." He said.

I knew that he didn't know that I was the cause of him being here in the first place, not that it would have made a difference. However, I'm sure he didn't know I was working the hose with one of his buddies, which if even temporarily, made me one of their own. I didn't argue. I went back to the fireman on the hose and told him my predicament. He got more upset than I. I took the hose again and he went storming back toward the trucks. It wasn't very long before I heard one of the trucks start up, and another fireman come to relieve me from the hose. I went back toward my car. On the way, the fireman caught up with me.

The fireman said, "I apologize for the hassle. Again, I really appreciate the help. We rarely get civilians willing to do what you did, so there is no reason to penalize you by making you stay until the end. You have a good night buddy."

"You too, and thanks for clearing the road for me."

My mom was staying with me for a couple of days and she was up, wondering why I hadn't come home yet. I walked in the house.

"What took you so long to get home from school? I was starting to get worried." Mom said.

"Sorry I'm late, but I was...." I started to say.

"Where have you been? You smell like smoke and you look like you got a tan."

"Well Mom, as I was coming home from school, and only just a couple of blocks away, I saw this smoke...."

I proceeded to tell Mom about the fire and what happened.

The radiant heat from the fire was so intense that I had gotten a first degree burn on my face. I knew the fire was hot, I just wasn't aware of the danger of a burn at that distance away from the flames. At work and school, the next day, everyone was asking, "Where did you go to get a tan?"

There was a second incident where I saw smoke adjacent to a person's home. I was traveling east on Manchester when I noticed smoke coming from the side of a small house. I pulled into the driveway to check it out. The house had a chain link fence around it, about seven feet high. This was the east side of L.A. and not the greatest of neighborhoods. The gate was locked. I didn't know if anyone was home, but a trash can was on fire and was scorching the side of the house. Any longer and it looked like the house would catch on fire. As I was contemplating on jumping the fence, another guy pulled up.

"What can I do to help?" He asked.

"There is a garden hose on the other side of the house. See if you can reach it and begin putting water on that trash can. I'll see if anybody is home," he said.

He and I both jumped the fence.

"Hey, anybody home? Your house is about to catch on fire," I began yelling.

No one answered for a good two minutes. Finally, a lady, must have been about 75 years old, came to the door.

"Your trash can was on fire and we didn't know if we were going to be able to put it out. Fortunately, we were able to put the flames out. Are you OK?"

"Yeah. I heard all this ruckus and it scared me. That's why I have the fence up. There's a lot of riff raff in the area and I got tired of them bothering my property."

"Wel,l we didn't mean to scare you. Just wanted to get the fire out and to make sure who ever lived here knew what was happening."

We made sure the fire was out and watered down the house to cool it off. Afterwards we went back to the lady.

"By the way, do you have a key to the gate or do we have to climb back over?"

Graduation

When I graduated from East L.A. I had made the Dean's List. I had all "A's" and one "B."

"Mel, I have had you in my class for all your math courses, I know you know the material. But I want you to know that I really anguished over the "B" grade I gave you. I was really relieved to know that the "B" was not going to take you off of the Dean's List. You know you missed an "A" by two percentage points. But maybe I shouldn't have told you that. You're a bright guy and I expect to read about you someday. Always enjoyed having you in class." My Calculus instructor said

I had made a couple of errors on one major test that dropped my class grade. He wanted to find out what impact the "B" would have on

my grade point average and in doing so found out that I was on the Dean's List and would graduate Summa Cum Laude, even with the "B" in the class. He felt relieved. I didn't attend graduation. I had no one (maybe sis) that would come to see me graduate anyway. For our family, this was a milestone. No one else had a degree of any type, and for me, this was just the beginning.

A Strange Date

One weekend in L.A. a friend, Robert, and I went to pick up a couple of young ladies that my sister Dolores had asked if we wouldn't mind showing them around. We didn't mind. The name of the lady my friend had an interest in was "Natalie," and the name of the other lady was Tanya. We went to a couple discos that night. As the night wore on, it turned out that Natalie and I began dancing more with each other than she with my friend. By the time we made it to the second disco, there were no pretense that Natalie and I had more interest in each other than she and Robert. Oddly enough, Robert and Tanya were hitting it off pretty good. There was an unspoken transfer as Natalie and I continued to become acquainted, as did Robert and Tanya. Natalie and I saw each other several times after that and then she just disappeared for about six months. One night I ran into her at a party in Hollywood.

She saw me, ran up to me, kissed me, and said, "Mel daaalin', I missed you, where have you been?"

Natalie had changed. She had immersed herself in the Hollywood set and began to take on, to me, a faux personality. It was a good party; however, I didn't see much of Natalie as she was making her rounds; and in a sense "working" the party. It was obvious to me that she had chosen to do the Hollywood thing. That evening as I was leaving, I went to say good-bye to Natalie.

She hugged me and said, "Don't be a stranger."

As I left, I had a feeling that this night would be the last time that I would see Natalie. I am not one for the Hollywood set. My brother Wayne, a stuntman, always tried to get me involved in the Hollywood scene. Even with his continued encouragement I never had an interest. It wasn't long after that night that I heard that Natalie had landed a record deal. This was the start of her following in her father's footsteps, Nat King Cole.

Other Ski Seasons

As the next ski season progressed and we got better and better we ventured to other ski areas. There was Goldmine, Holiday Hill and Snow Summit, all within two hours of LA. In our second season, we found out that a Black ski club existed that would book trips to Mammoth Mountain, about eight hours north of LA. Larry and I met a couple of members and decided that we would try going on a trip with them to see if we liked it. Of course, the ski club was co-ed.

As the years went by, actually, near the end of the third season, I started skiing Black Diamond runs. Black Diamond runs were considered to be for expert skiers only. There are single diamond and double diamond runs. The double diamonds were obviously the more challenging. These runs would be steep, very steep with moguls, or "bumps" as skiers would call them. From this point on, my advancement in skiing slowed. Actually, it slowed in a purposeful way. I didn't take ski lessons for one simple reason. I liked my body. I knew that if I got too good, too fast, my maturity would not be able to keep up with my capability. I knew I would be out taking higher and higher jumps, doing helicopters (spinning while in mid-air) and doing all kinds of crazy stuff. As it was, by the time I was in my 5th and 6th season, I was taking jumps that were 8 – 10 feet high, and this was in my cautious state. Imagine if I was really, really good at this time period or even earlier. My enthusiasm for skiing was contagious as many of my friends began wanting to go.

Those that went, I would tell them, "I will spend two hours in the morning with you, teaching you the basics, after that you are on your own."

"Ah, Mel that's no fair, we may not catch on in two hours."

"OK, I'll come back in the afternoon, but understand this, I paid for a lift ticket to ski, not to instruct. It is unfair to me that I spend my money to spend the whole day with you, teaching you how to ski. Let's see what you can do in two hours."

I can't tell you the number of people that I have trained. At the end of the day, I would gather all together those that went skiing with us. Once we all were together, I would call out the first-time skier.

"Hey Sandy, would you mind stepping over here, I have something I would like to present to you. It is what I call our 'Snowflake' award. I give it to every first timer who successfully survives the day; and, you survived. Barely, but survived you did," I said with a smile.

I would buy these pins at a local ski shop just for these occasions. The reaction from the recipient was always priceless.

After a while I began to develop a skiing style that others said they could always tell that it was me. On many occasions, as I would ski the face, which often was under or close to the ski lift, which often was one of the steeper slopes, which often was the less skied upon, skiers in the chairlift would see me coming down the slope and I could hear them hollering "Hot Dog," a ski term that means appreciation. A far cry from our first day on the slope when Larry and I wiped out nearly everybody in line. I wasn't showing off, but I had been told my style of skiing was smooth and seem to be effortless. Oh course, whenever I could, I didn't mind "struttin' my stuff." On one such occasion, I had a day where it was probably the best ski condition I ever had. It was at Vail Colorado. It was a picture-perfect day. By now I had graduated to multiple ski outfits. I had a marine blue jacket, matching pants with a bold yellow two-inch stripe coming down each arm and on each side of the legs. I also had a matching color head band and cap. So, as I stood at the top of this black diamond run, dressed in my matching outfit, I no longer looked like a beginner. I did my mental exercise to picture the route that I would take.

This run crisscrossed under the chairlift, so I knew I was going to have an audience. Off I went. From the beginning, I knew I was going to have fun on this run. This run had bumps, plenty of bumps. There are many ways to ski the bumps, but for me on this day, with the conditions as they were, it was… "Showtime." I hit the bump, and instead of carving around it or going through the trough or between them, I went over the top. Airtime. While in the air, I set my skis, relaxed my legs to absorb the shock of landing, and came down the backside… one mogul over. I was jumping the bumps. Hitting the face, getting air, going over a bump, coming down, hitting the next bump, getting air, going over a bump, coming down. I did this over and over. Very quickly I was hearing all kinds of noises coming from the chairlift. They weren't just saying "Hotdog", but whatever they could think of to show their appreciation. I knew I was looking good and feeling it too. Now in a ski outfit a person is fairly well covered from head to toe. So, I reckon, many of the people in the chair had no idea that it was a Black guy of which they were cheering. Not that it would have made a difference. Even had they known, I'm certain the cheers would still be there. Maybe even more, in the sense of "Wow, a Black guy skiing like that!" The point here is I'm sure it would have been a surprise as people of color still were rarely seen on the slopes, let alone one on a black diamond run; and showboating at that. It was a great day.

After about two runs on this slope, I had a fellow approach me and said, "I saw you skiing under the chair, you were looking really good. Would you mind giving me a couple of pointers?"

"Don't mind at all" I replied.

On one other skiing trip, at Lake Tahoe, my date and I went to see the 5th Dimensions at one of the hotels. One of the members, Lamont McLemore, had a crush on my sister Vic when we were growing up, so I got to know him fairly well. My older brothers Wayne and Charles belonged to this social club called "The Playmates." Lamont would come to some events, but especially the beach parties. Myself and a couple of my friends were much younger but was adopted by the group. We often would be in the background being the DJ or playing bartender. On occasion, they would have these beach parties, at Playa del Rey, that would go all night. The group would have bongos, congas, castanets, tambourines, and all kinds of other percussion instruments.

The highlight of the night would be the Limbo contest. By the time this contest was held, a few cans of beer had been consumed by most of the club members, so the contest sometimes got a little rowdy. Because of the beat of the drums, the rhythm, and the beer, it inspired some of the girls to get down and dirty while going under the Limbo stick. Some of them became quite bold in their actions, but also remorseful the next day. A few of the guys would participate, but it was more a show for the ladies. And a show they put on. I would join the fray when the bar got fairly low and, in most cases, would end up winning, if there was such a thing as winning. It was more about watching the ladies than being serious about Limbo.

Fast forward a few years later. As I watched the 5th Dimensions come on stage, imagine my surprise when they began to put up a Limbo set, in Lake Tahoe. And wouldn't you know it, they were asking for volunteers to come from the audience. The ushers never got to my section, so I volunteered myself, and joined the rest of the people going up on stage.

As I came on stage and Lamont saw me, he exclaimed, "Mel, what are you doing here?"

"I came to see my favorite group." I responded.

We talked a little as the others started going under the bar. The bar got to be just above waist high when Lamont and I both noticed.

"Well, I better join the fray," I said.

We shook hands and he pushed me toward the Limbo line. Actually, going under a Limbo bar was a little difficult for me at a certain height. It was like a transition point where I would have to change positions; and this was that transition point, just about at waist level.

There was a tense moment for me while going under, until I heard Lamont call out, "Come on Mel, you can do it."

I did make it and now I was OK. They dropped the bar about two inches, which was just fine by me. The drop-outs happened very quickly at this point. The bar was lowered again. Soon there were three of us. The first person didn't make it. Two of us remained. The second person attempted, held her bent backward position for several seconds and then fell. I looked at the bar looked at Lamont and smiled.

I started my approach when Lamont says, "Wait."

He then comes over and very dramatically, takes the bar, looks at the audience, holds the bar above his head and then puts it on a lower notch. The audience loved it. I looked at Lamont, he looked at me, gave me this big toothy grin then he winked. OK, the challenge is set. I start my approach again. I'm going down. Just as my knees come underneath the bar, I realize I am in trouble. I am wearing a Nehru jacket and had it buttoned up. It felt like a straight Jacket. In all the excitement, I never thought to unbutton or take the jacket off. So now I am bent backwards, knees just under the bar. In Limbo, once the knees go under the bar, a person cannot back out, if they do, they are then disqualified. So, I started doing the one thing I should have done; and, what would permit me to have the freedom I needed. While still under the bar, I started to unbutton the first of about eight buttons. Florence LaRue saw what I was doing came up behind me and very sensually, began unbuttoning the rest of the buttons. At this point the audience began clapping their hands and screaming. Florence slowly removed my jacket as she ran her hands down my arms and back. Florence was really milking this. The audience jumped out of their seats and the screams got louder. Finally, with a flourish, Florence made a show in folding the jacket. I'm thinking, "Hey, uh, I'm stuck down here. I'd like a little sympathy, Thank you."

Fortunately, I didn't get a cramp as I remained in the one position. Finally, I continued under the bar. As I came up on the other side, Lamont was the first to congratulate me.

"Mel, that was great. Had no idea this would go over as it did. But you made it happen." Lamont said.

Florence came up to me, once again making a show of her interaction with me. She came close, looked me in the eyes, took control over my body and spun me around.

"Put your arms out," she said.

I extended my arms and she slid my coat up my arms and onto my shoulders. She spun me around again. With this action, the audience was on their feet again. They liked that I was being manipulated, like a puppet on a string. Florence finished the affair by slowly buttoning the jacket. She starts at the top and begins to work her way down. As she is going, she is building an anticipation in the audience. I never thought "buttoning" anything could be sensual. Unbuttoning, yes, but buttoning? When she gets to the bottom button, her fingers linger just a little bit. . . then she turns me around and pushes me away. The audience loved it.

Lamont came over to me. "Glad you came on stage, again, that was great."

I was escorted off the stage and as I was going back to my seat, many people in the aisle seats would jump up, slap me on the back or just say, "Way to go!".

For the rest of the week, I was surprised by the number of people that had seen the 5th Dimensions and were there the night that I participated in the Limbo contest. While on the slopes at Heavenly, many skiers would approach me and ask, "Are you the guy that did the Limbo?"

Then again, there were not many people of color on the slopes, so I guess the odds were in their favor.

American Spirit

On one ski trip, Rick, Doris, Renee, and I were leaving Vail and heading back to Denver. It had snowed all night and was still snowing when we woke up that morning to leave. As we got on the highway to leave Vail, it looked like the whole town was evacuating. The snow had stopped falling by now and visibility was pretty good, so we could see a long line of cars ahead of us very easily. As we were creeping along, we talked about the highlights of the ski trip and when we would come back again. Then, for no apparent reason, clear sky, little to no wind, we came to a halt. Rick was driving so I got out of the back seat to go and check out what was causing the hold-up. The road we were on was one of the highways that essentially crossed the "Continental Divide." All rain that fell west of the summit eventually flowed to the Pacific Ocean, and all rain that fell east of the summit went to the Atlantic Ocean or the Gulf of Mexico. What was happening, and due to the snow, that fell all night, the big rigs couldn't get over the summit. Front wheel or four-wheel cars were able to make the pass, but any rear wheel, semi's, or just about anything larger than a car or SUV, wasn't going to make it over.

I went back to the car and told Rick what I had seen. I also told him that I would be back as I was going to help, but he was to keep moving the car along with the traffic.

"Wait a minute Mel, you said help, what do you mean help?"

"You wouldn't believe this, but I think, what is happening could only happen in America. Guys are getting out of their cars, about 25 right now but more are coming, and they are pushing trucks and cars over the summit to get to the other side. It is all downhill from there."

It was amazing seeing 100 guys or more alongside a logging truck, acting as one, pushing this big monster uphill. Of course, the trucks would be turning their wheels to help, but it was the manpower that was needed for it to move, and move them we did. Up here on the summit it was cold and the wind started picking up. We had to get the big rigs over in order for the cars to go, it was only two lanes at this point. And because the rigs were sliding sideways, sometimes we had to be careful not to get caught under the wheels. Fortunately, there were no cars coming up the hill as apparently all traffic had been stopped at a lower level.

With the wind picking up, the wind chill started dropping, so we had to take turns being out in the cold. As progress was made, some of the guys had to hitch a ride with other families because the car they were riding in had gone over the summit. People were opening their car doors and letting strangers in. It didn't matter, we were Americans, and we were skiers. When we got to the summit, Rick was out helping and I was driving the car. I blew the horn for Rick to come to the car and he barely made it as we crested the summit. If he had missed us, he would have gotten into the next car coming. As we proceeded down the mountain about 10 miles, we saw a roadside look-out spot where people were pulling over and exchanging passengers. What just happened, and of which we were a part of, could not have worked better had it been planned. I was really proud of my country and the folks in it that day.

A Picnic

Prior to graduating from East LA, I had to take a required Speech class. To keep on my schedule, to meet my goal in 12 years, I signed up for a summer course in speech at West LA Junior College. All of us in the class got along so well that we decided to have a picnic at Griffith Park, on a Saturday, at the end of the course. I acted as coordinator for the event; and just to be on the safe side, in case no one showed up, I invited some of my friends to come as well. Larry showed up with his family, along with several others. In total, we had a little more than 15 people at the picnic. Only one person from class, Buglioso, we called him "Bug" showed up. The day actually turned out to be a lot of fun, so much so that several people requested that I coordinate a picnic for the upcoming Labor Day weekend. I took on the challenge and expanded the invite list. This was the beginning of our twice a year picnics, Memorial and Labor Day weekends. The size of the crowd grew from the 15 plus, to over 250 by the time I left LA. A couple of other friends and I would arrive at the park at 7:30 AM on Saturday, reserve tables and volleyball courts, and try to define and cordon off locations for our group. The unwritten rule was, bring something and put it on the table or, as we got bigger, tables as in "many" tables. There was no hoarding or separate eating tables. The only food that was permitted for private stash, were ribs. We knew that ribs, if they were put out on the table, would not last until lunch and neither would the person who brought them get any. So, stashing ribs was permitted.

The whole day was active. We would start out playing baseball in the morning, followed by several games of volleyball, break for lunch, another game of baseball, more volleyball and then the grand finale, tackle football. Football would always begin somewhere around 5:00 PM and would close out the picnic. Meanwhile, there would be continuous games of Bid Wisk and Checkers being played. The entertainment, well that is a story in itself. By the third picnic, my brothers, Charles and Wayne, and a few of their friends, who brought bongos, congas, tambourines and a few other percussion instruments, would set up and would begin playing right after lunch. They would have an all-day jam session. It created such a lively atmosphere that other picnickers began to mill around and hang out. By the fourth year, I began to look for another park in which to hold the picnic. Griffith was getting to be too congested for the 75 - 80 people we had attending.

One day my sister Vic and I took a ride out to a park just south of LA, called El Dorado. It had several baseball diamonds, volleyball courts and plenty of picnic tables scattered around, and a play area for children. The layout was much better; and permitted those not participating in baseball or volleyball the ability to see the action from the picnic area. When we moved to El Dorado, attendance doubled in size within the next two years. The Jam sessions became a mainstay that now included saxophones, flutes, horns, electric guitars, (yes, someone brought out a generator for electricity) and a huge set of speakers. An electric piano later joined the group. The park was extremely large. However, because of the music, groups that came on the days that we showed up would make sure they got tables fairly close by. Some would even join up with us. By the time we had the last picnic, in 1985, we had over 250 people attending. The picnics ended in 1985, because that was the year we moved from LA to Orlando. It was unfortunate that no one else was willing to take over the coordination.

As I look back on that time, and the number of people that were getting together, from all walks of life, ages, social economic standing and nationalities, I am amazed that we didn't have any fights or arguments. I believe one reason for that was, everyone knew, that if you started an argument, you were not invited to the next picnic. It was self policing. I remember the days being fun with wholesome interaction with family and friends, but not recognizing at the time how unique the experience was. It all started from a summer school speech class.

Interviews

Aero Jet started having some financial difficulties that became apparent to me, so, along with many others, I began looking for other employment. I remember one interview with Xerox. I went to the place where Xerox was conducting the interviews and met the gentleman, Bill, that I spoke to on the phone. He had some things that he had to do, so he asked his assistant to administer the test that they give to all potential technician type applicants. I accompanied his administrator to a room and listened attentively as she gave instructions. The test would be timed.

When she finished, she said, "Good luck" and left the room.

At the time, I believe I was in my last semester at East LA, so I was use to performing to a timed test. I started going through the questions and found the test relatively easy. I completed the test and sat my pencil down. A few moments later, the admin came into the room just to check up on me. Time had not expired; she was just checking to see how I was doing. When she walked in and saw that I was just sitting there with the pencil laid across the test, she assumed the worst.

"Is there a problem, was the test too difficult?" She asked.

"No, I'm just finished." I replied.

The expression on her face was one of disbelief. "Did you answer all the questions? Are you sure you don't need more time?"

"Yes, I answered all the questions and I don't need anymore time."

She gathered the test and the pencil and said "Come with me."

I followed her out of the room and sat back down in the waiting area.

I heard her call Bill and say, "Hi Bill. Mel finished the test. (pause) Yes, he completed the whole test. (pause) Ok, I'll check the scoring and call you. She was quiet for a moment, then said to Bill, "I will inform him of that."

"Mel, something came up that pre-empted you meeting with Bill. Is it OK if Bill contacted you later on the phone? He really wants to speak with you," she said.

"Sure, I don't mind at all."

Since I had another interview scheduled this just gave me more time to get there and not be rushed.

The year was now 1972, I went to Hughes Aircraft Company (HAC) in El Segundo to meet a friend of my sister's, George, who in turn was going to introduce me to a former boss of his so that I may interview for a job. (At the corner of Sepulveda and Imperial Hwy. the cluster of buildings is now owned by Boeing and/ or Raytheon). I met George in the lobby.

"You must be Mel."

"And you must be George."

"Sure am. Your sister is quite a gal. Good worker and well liked. She told me you were in school, doing quite well, and have a good head on your shoulders."

"Were you talking to MY sister?"

"Hah, hah. Good to see the sibling rivalry going there."

From that exchange, George and I got on the elevator and road the elevator together to the fourth floor. We got out, went to the office of Mr. Oldham or Mr. "O," and I was introduced. Mr. O was a Section Head, in Finance, responsible for cost accumulation for the whole division.

"Hi George, haven't seen you in a while. And your friend here is…?" Said Mr. O

"Mr. O, this Mel King. He's the gentleman I told you about. Since he was coming to have an interview with you, I thought I would take this opportunity to come along to do the introductions; and, to see you."

"Glad you did George, as I said, it has been a while."

George and I accompanied Mr. O to his office and we both sat in chairs, facing Mr. O's desk. Since Mr. O had not seen George in a while, Mr. O was curious about what George was doing these days. As a result, the two of them began entering into a conversation. George had been promoted to a department manager so he and Mr. O had a lot to discuss, capturing all the things that George had done since leaving the employ of Mr. O. The two of them talked for about 30 - 35 minutes. I sat there just listening.

As the conversation wound down, Mr. O looked at me and asked, "Do you have a degree or are you attending school?"

"I am attending school, about to receive my AA degree, and I am on the Dean's List for graduation. I plan to continue towards my Bachelors next semester." I replied.

Mr. O looked at me for a few seconds, then looked at George and said, "Well, George, I know you and I both have work to do. Guess we better get back to it. Thanks, George, for stopping by."

George stood up and I followed suit. Mr. O and George shook hands and then Mr. O looked at me and said, "Glad to have met you."

With that the "interview" was over. I walked out of the office into the hallway with George.

As soon as we got in the hallway, George looked at me and said, "Congratulations on your new job."

"Job, what job? What about an interview?"

"You already had the interview, I am just not sure what the job will be, but you'll be hearing from someone soon."

"You mean the discussion you and Mr. O had was my interview?"

"Yep."

"Wow! How did you know he liked me?"

"For one, he asked you a couple of questions. Two, he liked your answers. Here's my business card. Give me a call the first day and I'll stop by to see you, good luck."

"Uh George, I have a question. Is that how it feels to be one of the 'good ol' boys.' Opportunities come at you without necessarily trying?"

"I hadn't thought of it that way, but yeah. Don't get used to it though. You are coming in at an entry level position, when you start to compete at the management level, it is a whole new ball game. Fortunately, I had Mr. 'O' as a mentor and he helped me a lot to get to the position I am in now. Without the mentorship, it is a hard road to travel."

With that, George turned around and walked away. I was dumbstruck, but boy was I glad. I didn't know what kind of job it was going to be, but I didn't care. I figured all I needed was to get in and prove myself. My mind was racing the whole time as I was driving home.

As I walked into my little one-bedroom apartment, the phone began to ring. I hurried over to pick it up. It was Bill from Xerox.

"Mel, I have been trying to reach you all day. Sorry about my being detained, but something came up and I couldn't get back with you when you were here. My admin told me about what happen when you were taking the test. That she walked in and you were just sitting there. She said she thought something was wrong, or that the test was too difficult or something. She was totally dumbstruck to know that you had completed the test. Not only did you complete the test in record time, you registered one of the highest scores. That's why I have been trying to reach you all day. Oh, by the way, how are you doing? I have just been rambling. Sorry about that."

"I am doing well Bill. I just came back from an interview with another company; and, I believe that I am going to get a job offer."

Bill jumped on that comment immediately.

"Well, that is the reason that I am calling. I want to make a job offer to you. I have an immediate opening for a service technician and I can get you here on the job and into training in three days."

"Bill, had we spoke earlier today, I'm sure you would have presented a great opportunity that would have been difficult to turn down. But now I want to wait until I hear from Hughes. Bill, I don't know what the job at Hughes will be. All I know is that it will be in Finance and I believe that it will be supportive of my quest for a degree; and career goals. A Service Technician would not provide me with any related experience toward a financial degree. Bill if you don't mind, I want to wait and see what Hughes will do before I give you an answer.

With that comment, Bill sweetened the offer, but I had to make the decision right then to get this new deal.

"Bill, in fairness to myself, I need to wait. However, if you still have the position open when I get back to you, I will accept your first offer since you were willing to wait."

"You decide to come our way I'll keep the second offer on the table, just so that you'll be thinking about it."

Bill was disappointed but said that he was willing to wait no more than three days. After getting off the phone with Bill, I immediately called George.

"Hi George. Let me tell you what just happened. Prior to my interview with Mr. O, I had gone to Xerox to take a test for a technician position. Evidently, I did very well and they are willing to hire me. The pay is good, the only problem is, it is not in the field that I want. I would much rather work at Hughes and with Mr. O. I told the person I interviewed with, his name is Bill, that I would rather work in finance, if the opportunity presented itself. When I told Bill that he said that he will keep the job offer open for three days."

"Ok, glad you called me Mel. I will see what I can do to help get an offer to you in three days."

On the third day, George called me.

"Mel, we ran into a little snag. It will take them about another two days to clear it up, however, they are working to get an offer to you. It is your choice to wait. There is no guarantee. They might, at the end of this thing, change the requirement, cancel the employment requisition, or who knows what. Are you willing to take the risk and wait?"

"George, is Hughes a good company to work for? Knowing what you know, would you work there again?"

"Yes, it is and yes I would." Said George.

"Then I will tell Bill at Xerox that I am going to accept the offer from Hughes. I'll just have to believe that I'll get the job."

"Mel, I'll see what I can do to make things happen."

I got off the phone with George with a sinking feeling in my stomach. I called Bill and gave him my decision. I just committed to turn down a job. Essentially, I traded a bird in the hand, for a bird in the bush. It wasn't even for two birds in the bush. What did I just do? Man, oh man. I hoped that there would be no regrets. There was a weekend during this time period of waiting. The only thing that helped to keep my sanity over the weekend was that I didn't change my routine. By this time, I was one week into unemployment. I was affected by the latest rounds of layoffs from Aero Jet. However, I still had school. I delved into the books and study as I never had before. It was all I could do to concentrate. When Monday came, I would jump every time the phone rang. I was a prisoner. I didn't want to leave my apartment and miss the one call I was waiting for. Monday came and went. Tuesday morning, the phone rang. I ran over to pick it up. It was Hughes.

"Yes, I can be there tomorrow by 8:00 o'clock to discuss the position you would like to offer me. Thank you. Good bye."

"Hallelujah, Hallelujah, Hallelujah."

Employment - Finance Associate

Wednesday, the following day, I met with Mr. O again. This time, he and I talked. He was an elderly man, in his sixties, and I found out later, highly respected within the company. Mr. O said that he would start me off as a Finance Associate making cost entries and tracking cost anomalies. He said he would start me off at $125 week. I was making $112/ wk at Aero Jet, so I did a quick calculation, huummm, just a little better than 10%, that's a no brainer. I would get paid for any overtime, although it would be rare, and Hughes pays every two weeks. I accepted the position. I would start the following Monday.

On Monday, I am introduced around and wouldn't you know it there were a couple of real cute girls in the office. I didn't mark them as a target, just persons of interest. I was shown to my desk and my supervisor, Gail, an oriental, jumped right in, showing me what I needed to do and how to do it. It was a good group, about eight of us working with Gail and about 20 - 25 in the whole department. Since computers only existed as main frames, many common and automated tasks of today had to be done by hand. My first assignment was to transcribe all the production charges from time clocks to these big, 11 X 17 ledger account books. This process was painstakingly laborious, but I was glad I had a job. There were several of us performing this transcription work.

Sometime during my second week on the job, Mr. O came back to our section, something he rarely did. He also was a man of few words. On this occasion, he had a ledger in his hand. All of us who were working on ledgers looked at each other. I had this sinking feeling. Two weeks on the job and I get fired.

Mr. O raised the ledger and asked out loud, "Who did this?"

Gail went up to Mr. O, recognized my writing and said, "Mel did the transcriptions of that ledger."

Mr. O looked at me and said, "Great job. The best I've ever seen."

With that he turned around and walked out. The whole office was stunned. This was an extremely rare occasion. Few had ever heard Mr. O give a compliment, and rarer in public. I didn't know to be embarrassed or proud.

Gail tried to lighten the mood a little as she said in a jokingly manner, "Well Mel, two weeks here and you get the first compliment ever, what are you going to do next week? Walk on water?"

With that, we all laughed and got back to work.

Although I was the only black person in the office, I was well received and after about a month, one of the two young ladies, her name was Yvonne, that I initially noticed, began to increase her communication with me. I never had a mentor, so no one ever told me about keeping office associations at a distance. I think both of us wanted to keep things discreet in case there was mutual interest, so we always made sure someone else was around when we got together at break or lunch. On one Saturday, there was an event I wanted to attend. I traded my Friday free night for Saturday study so that I may attend. I waited until an opportune moment came, when no one was around, and then I asked Yvonne if she would like to attend.

"Hi Yvonne. I have an event this weekend coming up that I thought you may be interested in. Problem is, you will have to go with me since I won't tell you where it is or what it is until you say yes."

"Well, I do have something to do. But I don't know what it is because somebody won't tell me what it is."

I was a little slow on the uptake.

"Oh, Ok. Just thought I . . . that is good. Very good." To my surprise, she said that she would love to go.

Then she tacked on, but with a smile, "I have nothing else to do this weekend."

"Make me feel good will yah." I responded.

We both laughed. We went out and had a great time.

I am not sure how a manager from Hughes Space division got my name, but one day I received a call. (The building that the manager worked in is located along side the LA airport on Imperial Highway. It is recognizable by the two radar domes. At the time of this writing, Boeing owned the facility.) This manager heard about me being a good worker, going to school at night, and wanted to interview me for a position in his department.

After the interview, he said, "Mel, I think you would fit in well with our organization. If you want the job, it is yours. Take a couple of days to think about it and let me know."

I went back to my department in Finance, only to discover everyone already knew about the interview and that the position had been offered to me. Never could understand how that rumor mill worked, especially so fast and accurately. The next day I was in the filing storage room by myself, cleaning, organizing, and just straightening things up.

Mr. O walks in, says, "Good morning."

"Good morning Mr. O," I said.

He looks at me and then says, "Some people just don't have enough patience."

With that, he turns and walks away. As I said, Mr. O was a man of few words. For the next 10 -15 minutes, I stood there processing his comment. Am I missing something? This other position amounted to a promotion with more money. But, will I miss something if I go? Would

Mr. O be a mentor, something that I never had? Was what he said a veiled promise? One thing I knew, Mr. O does not go out of his way unless there was a reason. Once again, I decided to let the bird in the hand go free. Not sure that I like making these kinds of decisions with little to go on. However, later that day I went in to see Mr. O, told him that I was not going to accept the other position. I then went out and called the other manager to inform him of my decision.

Hughes - Industrial Engineer

A month didn't go by before two significant things happened. One, I was given an opportunity to train as an Industrial Engineer (I.E.), and two, we found out that Mr. O was diagnosed with cancer and would retire immediately. It was obvious to me that he knew something was happening with him and that he set in motion to have me train to be an Industrial Engineer before he left. He was keeping his implied promise. It was a sad day for all of us to see Mr. O leave. I asked him if I could call him sometime, and surprisingly, he gave me his phone number. Over the next few months, I did give Mr. O a call and gave him an update on me and the office. The week Mr. O left, we were introduced to our new boss, a Mr. Fields. Over the next five - six months, I didn't have much interaction with Mr. Fields until I believed I was discriminated against.

When I was given an opportunity to become an Industrial Engineer (I.E.), the company hired Kevin, a young college graduate with an I. E. degree. We both went through the same training and progressed equally in our performance. By the fourth month, I had a couple of programs, one being the F-15 radar assembly line, of which I had responsibility. I would do "Motion Time Measurements," or MTM-3 as it was called, to determine how long it would take to put sub-assemblies together. We would use this time, along with a log-log scale to estimate the hours it would take to build each component. We would add each component to get the total time for the assembled radar. The Program Manager, (whose name also happened to be Mel) and I got along really well. Often times when he saw me on his line, he would call me into his office and just talk. Rarely would it go less than five minutes, I think he just liked that I was a good listener. After about six months at performing I. E. work, Kevin got promoted. I didn't. I went to my supervisor to ask why I was not promoted as well.

"Kevin got promoted because of his degree." My supervisor said.

"I know Kevin was paid more than I when he first started. I know that was because he had a degree and I didn't. I have no argument with that. However, when he and I go through the same training, perform equally well, we do the same function equally as well, and he gets promoted and I don't, something is wrong; and, I would like to talk with someone about it, if you are unable or unwilling to fix it," I said to my supervisor. "I'm not arguing about the salary differential at the onset, as I said, I understand that. He had a degree and I didn't. Now however, we should be judged equally if we are performing the same work."

What I didn't say was, "I know he's White and I'm Black."

Did I think this was a factor, yes, but I wasn't going to go there. I believed my performance should speak for itself; and hopefully carry the day. My supervisor was taken aback by my request and determination to have this thing "fixed". After all, I had never exhibited this type of bold behavior in the past. My supervisor went in to talk to Mr. Fields. A short time later he returned and said that there was nothing he could do. I then requested an audience with Mr. Fields. The supervisor left, returned and said the next open date on his calendar was next week. I said I didn't want to wait that long and that I am requesting an audience with the company controller, since that was who our department ultimately reported to. The supervisor left again and said that Mr. Fields would check the controller's schedule. As I look back on my life, there are times when I have been extremely bold, ignorant or stupid. A coin toss could probably decide the difference. The controller of Hughes, in today's vernacular, was the Chief Financial Officer (CFO) for the division of about 15,000 people. I was new to the company with little experience that, if I left or they fired me, would have no impact on the company and yet, I had the audacity to request an audience with the CFO. Still, I thought I was right in what I believed; that I was treated unfairly. I was willing to defend my position but I also knew there could be adverse consequences.

The following day, Mr. Fields finally called me into his office to speak with me face to face, rather than going through the supervisor.

"Mel, I spoke to the Controller about meeting with you, however the Controller wants me to resolve whatever issue you may have. I can meet with you but because of my schedule it will have to be after hours." Darn, that would interfere with my travel to school, but this was important. I agreed to do so. That evening with Mr. Fields I expressed my disappointment and presented my argument as to why I believed I was deserving of a promotion as well. For the next 3-4 evenings, we talked for about 45 minutes each evening. We were going no where. On the fourth or fifth evening, Mr. Fields had an epiphany moment. He just started laughing and laughing. I had no clue of why he was laughing or what I said that caused him to laugh the way that he was. Finally, he slowed down enough to speak.

He looked me in the eye and said, "You think I am full of bull- - -- don't you?"

I just looked at him and smiled. He finally got it.

"Now that we are beginning to understand one another, maybe we can make some progress." Mr. Fields said.

There was a noticeable difference in the conversation from that moment on.

He summarized in 15 minutes, four days of conversation by saying, "Here is what I am willing to do. I will give you two support personnel that you will supervise to help you with an expanded assignment. After two months, I will speak with all the Program Managers that you work with and get their assessment of your performance. If at the end of that period, and all is well, I will give you that promotion. I agreed to the terms. At the end of the two months, I got the promotion, along with a salary increase. Three months later, Hughes was coming out with their annual merit adjustment. I was called into a conference room by Mr. Fields with five other supervisors. He had checks that represented pay increases for us and the people of which we supervised. After he spoke a little about the company and the department, he began handing out the checks for us, and those that we were to give to our people.

As we stood up to walk out, Mr. Fields said, "Mel, please stay, I would like to speak with you."

A little puzzled, never-the-less, I went back and sat down.

Mr. Fields said, "I want you to know I did something I have never done before. I even had to go to the Controller to get permission. In fact, the Controller questioned me about this because he remembered your name from the time you requested to see him."

Oh boy. It is true, things that you think are dead and buried can come back to bite you.

"Mel, after your promotion, when I went back to check with the Program Managers on your performance, they all couldn't say enough about what you do for them. I knew I would have egg on my face when I spoke to the Controller. However, I learned something from you. With you, and because you believed in your cause, it didn't matter who it was you had to speak to; you were willing to take it to the end. You deserve the recognition and I took it on as my cause. So here is your check. It is a 20% raise. I kept it from the other stack I was handing out because I wanted to talk to you personally. Congratulations."

I was dumb struck. With that increase, I was making about $180 a week (this was big money in those days, especially for someone without a degree. Later in life, as an Executive VP, I made that much every two hours). In just over a year I increased my salary by 38%. What Mr. Fields found out was, "Black can make a difference."

From Trash to Gold

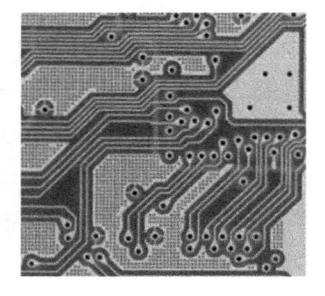

One day I was conducting a motion-time-measurement (MTM)study in the Printed Circuit Board (PCB) Department. From Wikipedia, "A printed circuit board (PCB) mechanically supports and electrically connects electronic components or electrical components using conductive tracks, pads and other features etched from one or more sheet layers of copper laminated onto and/or between sheet layers of a non-conductive substrate. Components are generally soldered onto the PCB to both electrically connect and mechanically fasten them to it." Here, in this department, the circuit boards are coated with a fine layer of gold, which ultimately will be the electrical circuit for the small chips or other components. The gold is then covered with a non-conduction material that will protect the board. Next, the circuit design (routing of the electrical circuit) pattern is adhered to the top of the PC board. Then the board is subjected to a hydrochloric acid wash. The acid removes all the gold, except where the circuit design pattern protected the gold underneath. This will be the electrical circuit. The waste from this process is highly caustic and is kept in five-gallon carboys.

While there I casually asked the department manager, "What do you do with the waste that contains all the gold?"

"We call a waste management company and they come and pick it up for us." He responded.

"Do they charge us for removing the carboys?

"Oh yeah. We pay an extra fee because of the hydrochloric acid content, and the potential impact to the environment."

I continued on with the MTM study, but something was percolating in the back of my mind. Later that day when I returned to my desk, I started making a few phone calls. I found this one company, a Borax mining company.

"Hello, I'm calling from Hughes Aircraft Company, and I would like to know if your company can help us. We etch printed circuit boards using hydrochloric acid and put the waste from this process in five-gallon carboys. Can you help us in reclaiming the gold?" I asked.

This company was more than glad to work with us. They ended up coming to Hughes, picking up the carboys, filtering the gold, paying us for the gold extracted, less their expenses, and sending back the carboys for further use. The mining company was glad to get the business, and Hughes no longer had to pay to remove highly caustic material, but got money back instead. It was a "Win/ win," for both companies.

I don't know what the total savings was, but cumulative, over a year with the number of PC boards we were making, it had to have been in the tens of thousands of dollars. I'm sure the waste management company, that was charging to remove these carboys full of gold, was very disappointed when Hughes cancelled the contract. They, themselves, were probably extracting the gold and charging Hughes to get it. And I am sure, by now, you know what I got in return, a polite "Thank you" and maybe a paper award. Something like a $500 check would have been great, especially in that time period. It would have been huge to me, but a vey small fraction of the savings. After all, no one asked me to look into the "waste" and to Hughes, it was found money.

A Vacation

I was at the six-month mark with Hughes and I had a week's vacation coming. I bought a new car about two months ago, a Mazda RX-3, in today's terms it would be called a "Pocket Rocket." It had the new Wankel rotary engine and could really fly. Having a new car, I decided to drive to Denver to see Rick and his wife. Rick is the officer I met at the Air Force Academy with whom I developed a close friendship. I would be remiss if I didn't say that I would be seeing Dee during this trip as well. I set out on my journey around 8 O'clock on a Thursday night. I had to let some of the LA traffic disperse since I was heading east on the 10, or San Bernardino Freeway (We Californian always put "the" in front of the highway number), which is like a parking lot from about 4 – 7 PM. I filled my gas tank earlier that day and did a little running around but did not cap it off (this was very significant later). It was one of those occasions when your subconscious tells you to do something, and you ignore it. As I left LA, I passed through the city of West Covina. There were several gas stations alongside the freeway with "easy off, easy on" signs. I ignored them all. The first stop on my route was Las Vegas. There I would fill up and continue my journey. Las Vegas is about 270 miles from LA and I figured I would get there somewhere around midnight. I was making good time when about 30 miles out from Vegas, I heard a clicking sound. I turned the radio down so that I could hear better. After all it was a new car and I didn't know all the peculiarities just yet. Just as I turned the radio down, the noise stopped. Humm. I keep the radio low in case the noise repeated itself. As I began to ascend one of the low-lying hills, I heard the sound again. I looked at the gas gauge it was registering a quarter of a tank. Wonder what that noise could be. It ceased once I got on top. By now I could make out the glow of the Vegas lights. I thought that I may end up wasting a whole day if I have to stop by a mechanic's shop to figure out the problem. May have to wait until the morning; but at least Vegas was close and a mechanic would be available.

As I ascended the next hill, the sound came again. Oh no, gas. I was hearing the fuel pump. The gas gauge was not accurate. Evidently the fuel pump was located at the front of the tank, so every time I went uphill it was starving. I went up the hill, turned off the engine on the downside and coasted. Turned on the engine to ascend the next ridge, turned off the engine on the downside. I repeated this process until I got over the last ridge. There it was, Vegas; and about 12 miles of flat land. Do the math. Vegas is 270 miles from LA, I had a 14-gallon gas tank; and I just found out that I get about 19 miles to the gallon, or about 266 miles per tank. Also, I did a little running around before I left LA. Had I stopped and filled the tank in West Covina, I would have had enough gas to get to Vegas before I ran out. I put on my emergency flashers, slowed to about 40 mph, and kept looking at Vegas, trying to will it to come closer. Alas, the clicking sound came on again. The engine died. I pulled over onto the side of the road. I got out of the car and stood near the front of it. It wasn't too long before a couple in a VW bus pulled over to see if they could help. (These were the days when people still tried to help others - without fear of being robbed, killed, or sued.) As I was explaining to them what had happened, a Nevada State Trooper pulled up. He came up to join us.

"Good evening, folks, what's the problem? The trooper said

"This is a new car, the gas gauge showed I had a quarter tank, but evidently the tank is empty."

He said, "I can help you with that."

With a looked of surprise on my face, the trooper chuckled.

"Are you from L.A.?"

"Yes. How did you know that?"

The trooper said, "We get a lot of people from LA, on their way to Vegas and they run out of gas. Of course, Vegas wants those people to arrive, without delay, so they equipped our cars with a pump. I can pump a few gallons of gas into your car to get you to Vegas."

Talk about out of the box thinking. The city management didn't want poor planning to keep people from spending and losing their money in Vegas. The trooper put a few gallons in my car.

"How much do I owe you," I asked.

"Don't worry about it, I'll be recompensed when you get to Vegas. I thanked him, got in the car and thought, "What good fortune," as I continued on to Vegas. I filled up in Vegas and made a mental note, 250 miles, fill up. It would take about five fill-ups to get to Denver from LA. Gas was about $.35 a gallon at the time.

This is confession time. For the most part I am an honest, trust worthy person. However, on this one occasion, I had a little scheme to gain one extra day of vacation. I planned to call in sick, not sure what excuse I planned to use, but I was going to call in. I had not had a sick day since being at Hughes. So, in my immature thinking "they owed me one." I made one other stop around four in the morning to fill up. I wasn't going to run out of gas again. I was in the state of Utah. Pretty country, rather flat but had an interesting landscape, small population and…not very many gas stations. Around 7:15 AM I began looking for a gas station. I wanted to make the call into work around 7:45 AM and fill up with gas. Seven thirty came and went. Seven forty-five came and went. Now I am starting to sweat. I wanted to make sure I called before eight. Seven fifty-five, I see a little convenience store, no gas, but a superman type phone booth next to the road. I pull over, make the connection, called my supervisor at work. I began giving the sad story of not coming in, not feeling well, voice scratchy, and about then, a big 'ole, 18-wheeler comes up behind me and rumbles past, very loud, doing about 70 - 75 miles an hour. The telephone both shakes, rattles, and feels like it was going to blow over. That big sucker startled me, I can only imagine how it sounded on the other end of the phone.

It got quiet on the other end for a second, then the supervisor said, "Well I hope you get better so that you can enjoy your vacation." I tried not to stretch out the conversation as I saw another semi approaching in the distance. I figured he was about a half mile away, and with the speed they are traveling, I figured I had about 25 seconds to get off the phone. My supervisor said a few more words, but thankfully he said good-bye. Just as I hung up the phone, I could feel the vibration and hear the noise that the approaching semi was making. Whew, close call. Now to find some gas. Did I say that Utah was fairly desolate? I was on route 70 and I didn't see much of anything, not even gas stations. By now you may have noticed that I had this fixation about gas stations.

I was now in Colorado, making good time, doing about 75 mph. Posted speed was 70 mph. Getting close to the time where I needed to get gas. Suddenly, I noticed red lights flashing in the rear-view mirror. State Trooper. I pulled over. He came to the car, said he clocked me doing 75 in a 70-mph zone.

I started to say, "It must be a slow day" but thought that would probably tick him off.

"You know I'm going to have to write you a ticket" The trooper said.

I said "I want to protest the ticket."

"You will have to go to court to do that."

"That is fine. I am willing to do that."

"Then you will have to follow me."

I followed him into a small town, and into the courthouse. Surprisingly, there was a judge on the bench, wearing a judge covering. I pleaded 'No contende' or something like that, which I hope meant, "No contest." I wasn't saying I was innocent, but neither was I saying I was guilty. The judge permitted me to speak.

"Your honor, I'm not sure on the proceedings of the court, may I speak directly to the trooper? .

"Granted." The judge said.

"Trooper Jack, would you mind telling me how the radar works"

He said "The operation is fairly simple, turn on a few switches and point the radar gun."

"Does the gun have to be hand held?"

"Yes, unless it is mounted."

"Is the radar in your car mounted?"

"No, it is not."

"Then how could you have held the radar gun? When I saw you, you and two other troopers were out of your vehicles standing on the side of the road talking. How could you have known how fast I was traveling?"

With that question, the judge intervened. He said a few words, essentially dismissed the case, but said I had to pay $25 in court fees. I paid the fee. I left the courthouse and once again began looking for a gas station. I arrived in Denver late afternoon on that Friday.

Cal State Los Angeles

There is not much to say about Cal State LA other than it being very different from East Los Angeles Junior College. I enjoyed the instructors at East LA but found very few at Cal State in which I could say the same. At East LA, the instructors were primarily business people, teaching at night, so they had real world experience, most of whom I could relate. At Cal State, many of the instructors were full time professors and had little real-world experience. I got into a lot of heated discussions with many of the instructors since they were often teaching about theory and not about practical application.

My first semester at Cal State I met a young lady, who was a foreign exchange student, that was from Spain. She often sat on the periphery of a group of us, until one day I approached her.

"Hi, you look kinda lonely over here, all by yourself. Are you new to the school?"

"No, I am visiting your country on an exchange program, I am from Spain," she said.

"Spain, I always wanted to go to Spain. Is this your first semester?"

"Yes, it is."

"Well what is your name and why don't you come join us? I think we're pretty friendly."

Her name was Esperanza, she did join us, and did so thereafter. One unusual day L.A., traffic wasn't as bad as it normally is and I got to school early. I saw Esperanza sitting at our usual table, which by now, has been several weeks since I first asked her to sit with us. I walked up to the table and sat my books down.

"Hi Esperanza, what's happening with you this weekend?" I asked, only to be cordial. Esperanza was a little shy. I contributed her uncomfortableness to her lack of command of the English language.

"I'm going to a friend's party. Would you like to meet me there?" She asked.

Now this was a shocker. Esperanza never showed any interest, as there were often a group of us sitting at the table in the cafeteria studying and waiting for our classes. Perhaps she asked the question since it was probably the only time it was just the two of us at the table.

"That's a strange way to go to a party with someone. Meet you there?"

"Yes. I will be over a friend's house and she will take me to the party. I really would like for you to come."

"OK. Sure. What time and where?" She gave me the address and the time she expected she would be there.

I arrived at the party sometime after Esperanza.

"Hi Mel, When I didn't see you here when I came in, I didn't think you were going to come."

"Are you kidding, a beautiful young lady asks a guy to meet her at a party and he doesn't show up. The guy must be half dead or the guy must not like the opposite sex. I am neither. Thanks for inviting me."

Esperanza introduced me to a few of her friends as we began to know one another better. She was being very distant but engaging at the same time. I felt that there was some kind of dynamic playing that I didn't fully understand. However, Esperanza has a very nice personality and a good sense of humor. We both laughed about her choice of words sometimes, but that only added to the fun. As the night was coming to a end, Esperanza asked me a question.

"Mel, how would you like to come to Spain?"

"Spain, me, Spain? Spain is one of the countries that I have always wanted to visit. Why… why are you asking?"

"Over the past few weeks, I have been watching you, you are a good person. That is why I invited you to the party. I wanted some of my friends and family to meet you."

"Family? You have family here as well? You never introduced me to anyone and mentioned that they were a relative."

"I know, I didn't because I didn't want to make you nervous. You see, in Spain, I am a person, how do you say, a person of importance. I have several bodyguards here with me now, even when I am at school. They always keep their distance, but they are there."

"Wow. So how does that fit in with me going to Spain?"

"I want to ask my parents if it is OK if you came to Spain for a week or two and let me show you the country. But I had to get to know you better; and, I wanted some of my friends and family get to see who you are. Everyone here thinks you are really nice, and a gentleman. I heard no one complaining."

"OK... Now what?"

"I will check with my parents to obtain permission. I will let you know as soon as I can."

I continued to see Esperanza for the next week at the school cafeteria.

We really began to get along very well.

Near the end of the second week, I see Esperanza enter the cafeteria, head down, and walking rather hesitantly. It didn't look good.

"Hi Mel, I have some very sad news. I will be leaving next week to go back to Spain. I won't even be finishing the semester."

"Esperanza, what happened?"

"When I told my parents about you, and that I wanted you to come to Spain, they would have nothing of it. In fact, they were so angry that they said that I would not be able to complete the semester. What they were really saying and wanted was for me not to see you anymore."

"Esperanza, I have no idea who you are, except that you are very nice, a beautiful young lady, and from Spain."

"In our country, sometimes marriages are pre-arranged. I know that sounds strange in this day and time, but it is true, especially so if someone is a member of the ruling family. My parents were afraid that if you came to Spain and if something happened between us, then it would change all their plans for me. They said they could not let that happen."

"Their plans? What about your plans? Don't you have a say-so in your own life?"

"I know I never told you who I am, and I won't. But I will say that I am a member of. . . No, I won't tell you. Just know that my family is a very important family in Spain, and I must obey the wishes of my parents and the traditions of my country. Mel, I have to go now. My escorts have been waiting for me. I probably will never see you again, but I will always remember you."

With those words, Esperanza kissed me on the cheek, with a tear forming in her eye, turned and walked away. She never looked back.

I am left speechless, and now with a curiosity that may never be resolved. Who is this, Esperanza?

An Ungrateful Act

After about a year into my employment with Hughes, the company was planning on splitting off part of the manufacturing and assembly area and move it to a different location. They were looking for volunteers, so I volunteered to go. I knew the new division would have greater opportunity, and I liked the idea of a new challenge. However, I was denied the opportunity to go to the new division, due to a process I developed that helped to control manufacturing and assembly costs. (Once again, the company chose to ignore a contribution I had made instead of rewarding me for innovating thinking.)

As the months passed, I began to have a better understanding of my function in Industrial Engineering. I expanded my knowledge to where I could be more valuable to the Program Managers (PM) I served. With my studies in finance, coupled with my industrial engineering training, I developed a process where I could tie the projected manufacturing hours, with the average labor rate, to come up with a total manufacturing budget. This method proved to be fairly accurate and it wasn't long before the PMs, of which I worked, began using my method to control their programs. Individually they would call me into their office and we would go over each assembly area by assembly area to determine cost. The PM in turn would use this data to challenge the budget given them by Project Control (PC) if their analysis was different in a negative way. If it was favorable, then the PM would accept the budget provided by PC and plan for a cushion. All the PMs received a bonus if they brought their project under budget and an additional bonus if ahead of schedule. I in turn would develop Project Performance charts with my numbers for the assembly line. These charts were updated weekly and were displayed on the assembly line. They were like weekly report cards.

After being challenged repeatedly, one of the supervisors in PC, her name was Julie, asked a PM "Where are the PMs getting their budget numbers, they seem to be more accurate than mine."

One of the PMs showed her their worksheet that I put together for them and told her that I was working with them to develop the hours needed to complete the programs. Julie met with Mr. Fields (my section head) and asked if she could spend a few days with me to learn the process I was using. He agreed and I began showing her what I was doing. Julie quickly adapted the method to her budgetary process. At first the PM contested her numbers as before, until she showed them that she arrived at the numbers using the same technique that I used. After that, she began receiving wholesale acceptance of her proposed budget. It wasn't too long after my instructing Julie that the announcement was made to split the division. The PMs I provided support to were the same ones that Julie also supported; and, were the programs that were going to be split off to form the new division. Evidently the PMs had been speaking to senior management and informed them how they were able to keep better control of cost through the method I had developed.

The PMs that were not going to the new division wanted to gain understanding of this budgetary method as well (after all, if it could improve their bonus dollars, why wouldn't they want it). One day, while the split was still being formulated, and sides were being drawn, Mr. Fields called me into his office. He had a couple of other people in his office, one I knew, a PM. The three of them started questioning me on the budget process I developed and asked if I would be willing to train others.

Of course, I said, "Yes, no problem."

Being "Black can make a difference." There were no other Black individuals doing what I was doing, White either, but despite that, I was just pleased to make a contribution.

What I didn't know was that I had just sealed my fate. After about a half hour of further discussion I was dismissed to leave. The next day I was informed that my request to go with the other division was denied. The company wanted me to stay with the current division and instruct others on the budget process that I developed. Since I had trained Julie, she would be the one to go with the new division; and besides, they said, she is already in Project Control. Julie went with the new division; and, got promoted to a section head. Me, I got a thank you for being a good employee. Was I deserving of some recognition or reward, I thought I was. Was this action very ungrateful on the part of Hughes? I thought it was. I thought about General Olds once again when he said, "Civilians don't often appreciate nor reward leadership, innovation, or dedication. The service does and has recognized innate leadership in you; which, will not necessarily be so in the civilian sector where politics and envy can come into play."

Julie was ultimately promoted to a director with her own department. Me, nada.

A Lady named Renee

I mentioned that while at Hughes I had graduated from East L.A. and was now going to Cal State L.A. This campus was also on the east side of L.A. and Hughes was on the Southwest side of L.A. I asked Mr. Fields if I could leave work 15 minutes early to beat the traffic. In L.A., 15 minutes can mean an hour difference in arrival time. Since I was already coming in a half hour early Mr. Fields agreed. While at Cal State L.A., I met several friends who, like at East L.A., would arrive at school early and sit in the Business School lounge. It was here that I met Gil and a couple of other friends, one being Mike. Gil and I later became housemates. Cal St. LA was on a Tri-semester system which meant that we literally went to school year-round. It was the second Tri-mester at Cal State and about a month after Esperanza had left campus, when one evening Mike and I were walking from the Business Lounge to class. In the distance, we saw these two, very attractive young ladies approaching from the opposite direction. In slow motion, we scoped them up and down, liked what we saw from the front side, cute, nice stride, wearing tight pants that emphasized shapely hip and legs. As we passed, we turned to check out the backside. To our surprise, the two ladies had turned to look at us. I guess they were checking us out as much as we them. Mike and I smiled, tipped our heads, and continued walking. We both starting talking at the same time. Wow! Really foxy ladies. Best looking chicks we've seen since we've been coming to school. They remained the topic of our conversation until we arrived at class. We never saw the ladies again that semester.

The following semester, I took an economics course. Since I was already at the university, I often would go to my class a little early so that I could sit close to the front. I learned that if you showed interest in the class, and if you were on the boarder line of a particular grade, that interest can sway judgment and get you the higher grade. First day of class, I'm sitting near the front, off to one side, near the windows. One of the young ladies Mike and I saw last semester as we were walking to class, walks into the room and sits down one row over and one seat behind me. I was doing something and was completely unaware that she came into the room. The professor walked in but we had a few minutes before class started. I looked around the room to see if anyone was in the room that I knew and was surprised to see that same attractive woman. As I was looking at her, she looked up and caught my eye. I nodded and kept looking around as if to imply, you were worthy of a hesitation but not a stop. Just before the class started a rather tall black guy walks in the room gives her a hug and sits next to her. They know one another. OK, cross that one off.

From here I need to tell the story about the first day of Economics from Renee's perspective.

> *I forgot all about the guys we passed that evening, last semester, until I walked into my Economics class, and there sat one of the guys we saw. I purposely sat behind him and to the side, just so that I could observe his mannerism. He sure is studious. His head has been in that book and hasn't looked up since I sat down. The professor just walked in, let's see what happens now. Yea, he is looking up and around. He looks at me, a slight pause, a nod, and then continues to look around the room. The nerve of the guy, he hardly gave me any attention. Just as I was musing over what had happened, a friend of mine comes in the class gives me a hug and sits next to me. This exchange did not go unnoticed by "the guy." I thought, oh what great timing.*

The next week, I saw that same attractive woman again, this time in the Business Lounge area. I got her attention.

"Hi, my name is Mel, how 'bout joining my friend Mike and I at the table over there? I asked.

"Oh, OK," she said.

"What are your studies and how long have you been going to Cal State? I asked.

She joined us and we exchanged pleasantries, and of course our names. This young lady's name was Renee and she was majoring in Marketing. For the rest of the semester, she would join us at our table. I don't know where her guy friend was, the one in our Economics class, and I didn't ask. Occasionally we would walk to our Economics class together. By the third class, she changed her seat location to sit across from mine instead of slightly behind.

One day in class, as I was sitting next to the window, I noticed this fantastic sunset. I was so immersed in the wonder of nature that I totally forgot where I was.

I didn't rejoin the class until I heard the professor say "Some of us are more interested in sunsets than economics."

He shouldn't have said that. He called attention to what had me mesmerized. He lost the entire class. Now the whole class was focused on this gorgeous sunset. Fortunately, the professor had a sense of humor and let the class go on this nature journey for a few minutes before he called the class back together.

"Mel, may I see you after class?"

It was phrased as a question, but I knew it was not a question, it was a command. After class, I humbly received my lecture, with promises of not doing again what I did.

After the professor finished, he said, "It was a beautiful sunset, wasn't it?"

We both smiled.

As the semester progressed, I noticed that Renee and her friend were communicating less and less and that she began to meet me more regularly before class. I asked her about her friend. She said, "We use to go out on a date every now and then but that is becoming less and less."

"Why is that?" I asked.

"Well, he kind of offended me. I was struggling with understanding something in our economics class, and I turned to ask him to explain something to me. He said something that implied that I was stupid or something like that and he didn't really help much. Later when I asked you that same question, you took your time and explained it with such clarity, I got it. You didn't seem bothered at all with me asking the question."

I continued to see Renee before and after class. The last day of class I asked her for her phone number. She later told me she wondered why I never bothered to ask her for her phone number before. What she didn't know was that I just didn't have room for her. With school, work, and the ladies I did know, I didn't have time to add another in the mix. So, I had stretched it out for as long as I could. I think it was another two weeks before I called her. (I know this may sound strange in today's social inter-actions; that Renee actually waited for me to call her, and that she did not initiate the contact.)

Our first date was a dinner at Charlie Brown's in Marina Del Rey. I went by to pick her up at her mother and step dad's home. As she came out to get in the car, I opened the door for her. I think she was a little surprised. When we arrived at the restaurant, I went around and opened the door again. When she went to sit down at the table, I pulled back her chair.

Once we got settled, Renee looked at me and said, "Do you always do this on the first date?"

"Do what" I asked.

"Be such a gentleman," she said.

I chuckled.

"Nope. What you see is what you get, all the time."

We then focused on what we would order. I think Renee was testing me to see what kind of reaction she could get from me as she ordered Lobster from the menu, at "Market Price." I didn't bat an eye. The evening went well in spite of the bread crumbs I got all over the place. It was a mess. I saw Renee a couple of times thereafter, when, and I am not sure why it happened, but something happened that gave me the impression that she was a little more conceited or "stuck up" than she led me to believe. We were at Gil's home; I had moved in about two months ago. It was a three-bedroom home in the city of Inglewood, just south of LA. I went to kiss her and she turned her head slightly. OK. I get the message. Just friends. I can live with that.

Later that evening I took Renee home and said "Good-bye."

She may have not known it then, but my good-bye was literally a good-bye. I had no intentions of calling her again.

I am at work, it's been about a week and a half since I dropped Renee off at home, I have not seen nor spoken with her since, when the phone rings. I pick it up.

"Hi Mel, this is Renee."

I am quiet for a few seconds; I then returned the greetings.

"Hi Renee. I trust you are doing well?"

"You weren't going to call me again, were you?"

"No, I was not."

"Do you still feel that way? I think you would be missing out on a good thing if you don't call."

I thought, yep conceited alright. Something was happening the upcoming Friday and she wanted to know if I would like to go with her. I had not made arrangements for the weekend yet, so I thought I would give it one more try.

"OK. What time and where? I asked.

After I hung up the phone, I began to wonder the rest of the day if I had made the right decision. After all, I had enough ladies in my life that I didn't need to complicate it with one that would require, what I consider, high maintenance. Didn't want that, didn't need that. However, understand, Renee is a very attractive young lady and, on the surface, has a very pleasant personality. It was a little difficult to say "No." I remember one time, much later in our dating, we were at Universal Studios amphitheater, Renee was in a white outfit with a rakish white hat, when this white guy came up to me and said, "I just had to tell you, she is one heck of a catch."

I'm glad he didn't say it loud enough for her to hear, but maybe she did, Renee has excellent hearing. On another instance, I was at a party with Mike from school, just having a good time, dancing and talking. The gals outnumbered the guys and we were really circulating thru the crowd. Mike and I both saw a couple of cute girls that we thought we would begin spending more time with. Just as Mike and I were about to make our move, the front door of the house opens. Renee and one of her girlfriends walk into the house. The two of them got everybody's attention. They were looking that good. I had no idea Renee was going to be here. We were seeing one another but not heavy dating. She and her friend walk through the house, Renee sees me, walks up to me and kisses me. Foul. No fair. There went any chance I had in getting acquainted with anyone that night. Renee knew what she was doing. She was protecting her investment. Oh well, I reluctantly, yeah, right, reluctantly spent the rest of the evening with one of the most attractive girls at the party. Renee and I dated off and on for about four years.

On one of those dates, about one o'clock in the morning, we were leaving a party in Inglewood. I had just gotten in the car to take Renee home when we both notice this elderly man get out of his car. Obviously, a person getting out of a car does not necessarily warrant attention. But how this person got out of the car and his subsequent actions were mesmerizing. As he opened his door, he kind of tumbled out. Renee and I looked at each other, didn't ask the unspoken question, "How did this guy drive home" but continued to watch. The guy stumbled and weaved his way to the steps of his apartment like condominium. As he got to the steps, he studied them a while, knowing that this was some kind of obstacle that he had to navigate. He grabs the banister and attempts to put one leg on the step. Ain't happening. He tries again. Every time he put his foot on the step, his balance is such that it causes his foot to slide off. Once again, he ponders the steps, reaches down with both hands and puts one leg on the step. He continues to look to verify that it stayed. Viola! He grabs the banister and pulls his other leg up. Once again, he reaches with both hands and grabs his leg, raises it up and set it on the next step. Fortunately, there were only four steps. Any more steps, due to the resultant height, I would have begun to be concerned about his safety. Finally, he makes it to the top step and the walkway to the front door.

The front entryway was all glass, the door and two side panels. There was a little step up just prior to the front door, but by now he's got the routine down. No problem. The front door was a different story. He reaches for the handle and realizes the door is locked. Keys. Yes, keys. OK, where are those keys. After doing the Macarena for about 30 seconds, he finds his keys pulls them out and determines he has another challenge. Which one? Surprisingly, that was accomplished much easier than Renee or I thought. He got the key, looked at the keyhole, looked at the key. It was like, 'How am I going to get this teeny-weeny thing in that teeny-weeny thing?' He gathered himself together, shook his head, walked toward the keyhole, and missed by a mile. He backed up, started again and missed by a mile again. The third time, he got key in hand, aimed it like a gun, and approached the keyhole. This time he did at least hit the lock, but no prize. Finally, with hand on the doorknob, he lowers himself down to his knees. Key in hand, aiming, he hits just to the side of the keyhole, but closer than any time before. Encouraged by this successful close proximity, he makes a final adjustment and the key enters the lock. While still on his knees he opens the door, and since he had his hand on the door and the door was supporting him, he followed the door until he was horizontal. He pushed himself back up to his knees, grabbed the door again to help him balance and stood up. He pushed the door closed, turned around to walk down the hall. The hallway was about five feet wide. As it was, he bounced from one side of the hall to the other. I am convinced, if the hallway was any wider, he would not have made it. One thing about this guy, even in his condition, he was a fast learner. His room was on the first floor. When he got to his apartment, he got on his knees to insert the key into his door lock, opened the door and fell in. Renee and I thought that what we had just seen made the whole evening.

A Halloween Party and Other Happenings

One Halloween Renee and I decided to go to a party out near Marina Del Rey with Nate and his girlfriend. We dressed up in the 50's style of clothing. Renee raided her mother's closet, while I did what best I could. The party turned out to be a dance at a dance hall. It was well attended with most people in some kind of Halloween attire. As Renee and I were sitting at a table with Nate and his girlfriend, my brother Wayne came into the room. His attendance was a surprise. He was dressed as a Ghoul of some kind. He, being a stuntman, and since there were a few Hollywood folks in attendance, he was well received. He was playing the part, going around heckling the females in the crowd, until this one lady, dressed in a black dress, with black flowing cape pounced upon him. The dancing stopped, and everyone gave them space. In slow-motion a fight to the death (if a ghoul can be any deader) ensued. It was amazing. Everyone knew this was unrehearsed, yet the two of them was pulling this fight scene off as if they had done it a thousand times. The Lady in Black managed to get her cape over Wayne's head, and with that, was able to get him to the ground. Once on the ground, she straddled him, removed her cape and bit him in the neck. Wayne convulsed in making one last try to recover, but to no avail. As he lay there on the floor, the Lady in Black looked at her prey, and then looked around the room, daring anyone to challenge her. Everyone clapped and cheered. It was a great impromptu performance. People went back to dancing.

About 20 minutes later we heard this laughter and more cheers. We obviously were wondering what was happening now. As the crowd parted, we saw the Lady in Black, chain around Wayne's neck, leading him around as her prized possession. Where they got a chain is anyone's guess. It was really great. That was the best Halloween party I had ever attended and it was the last.

Every Friday evening Renee, Gil, my sister Victoria, Ted, and others would go to play volleyball in the Inglewood gym. We would play from seven until 10 PM. Afterwards, we would go to Pann's restaurant on La Brea and Centinella. I believe the waiters and waitresses looked forward to our coming. We were a lively group, did not use any bad language, and did not get really, really loud. We went so often that the restaurant management began to reserve a special section for us. The interaction of the group was very dynamic and would change from week to week, depending on who came to the restaurant with us.

One Friday was special in that my sister, Victoria, got picked on big time. There were four or five of us in a booth, myself, Renee, Victoria, Ted, and Ted's friend. It's important to note that Renee was sitting next to Vic with Ted on the other side as our meal arrived. Vic had ordered a fish sandwich that we all voted as the best meal of the group. It was a rather large piece of fish that extended quite a bit beyond the bun on either side. The waitresses often would make sure that we were taken care of. As we began to eat our respective meals, Ted began to engage Vic in conversation. As Vic would turn to face Ted, sitting on one side of her, Renee would take her fork and cut off a piece of fish. It wasn't long before the folks at the other tables were witnessing this exchange. Ted would purposely distract Vic; Renee would whack off another piece of fish. When the giggles started, Vic became suspicious. It is known with the group, that if something funny is happening and you are not laughing with everyone else, then you are probably the target. Vic picked up on the giggles.

"What's happening? What are you guys doing?" She said.

One of the girls in another booth said, "Vic, how's the fish?"

With that comment, Vic took inventory.

"You little sneak." Vic says to Renee and turns the other way and hits Ted on the arm. "That's why you were talking. I was wondering why you were talking so much." The waiters and waitresses saw what was happening and joined in on the laughter.

Later, we ordered dessert. Vic and Renee were sharing a chocolate something when I noticed Vic had chocolate on the side of her mouth.

"Vic, you got a little chocolate on the side of your mouth," I said.

The napkin she used had a little chocolate on it, so when she wiped her mouth, she actually put some chocolate on her face. Ted jumped at an opportunity for payback when Vic had hit him earlier.

"Now you got some on your cheek." Ted said.

"Did I get it?" Vic said.

"No, now you got it on your nose."

Unbeknownst to Vic, every time she would go to the place that Ted told her to go, she was putting chocolate on her face, not taking it off. The giggles started again. The light clicked on. Vic was on Ted again. This time she was hitting him with both fists. The whole side of the restaurant erupted in laughter.

One of the waitresses said, "That's why we like having you guys come in. You're so much fun, and its clean fun. We really enjoy waiting on you."

Mazda RX-3

The Mazda I owned could tell a few stories of its own, however since it is no longer around, I'll have to tell them. The first thing centers around a peculiar trait of the Mazda that sometimes, when I take my foot off the gas – it backfires. Remember, this is a rotary engine, newly developed, so I guess all the bugs were not out of it. One thing for sure, the car could really fly. It was late at night, a lot of cars on Hollywood Blvd., mostly cruisers. I was in the left lane and traffic was crawling. I so wanted to get further down Hollywood Blvd. faster than what I was currently going. As I approached the next block, there was a little opening in the traffic, that if I hurried up, I could make the turn before someone changed lanes and closed the gap. I accelerated, got in the right lane and made the turn. As I turned, with my foot on the gas, unto the small side street, with its tall buildings and straight walls, I saw two cop cars. There were four cops, two were patting down two guys that they had up against the wall, the other two cops were standing back, hands on their weapons. I had been accelerating as I made the turn and instinctively, as we all do when we see cop cars, I took my foot off the gas. Wouldn't you know it. The car backfired. With the narrow street, nighttime, and the tall flat walled buildings, the backfire was unusually loud. All four of the police officers went for their gun and turned around to find the source of the "shot." Me, I accelerated once again made the next corner and got outta Dodge. I felt sorry for the two guys on the wall. I'm sure the cops were not in a very good mood after that little bit of excitement.

On another occasion, coming back from Hollywood, Renee and I were traveling down Highland Blvd. In the next lane, a fella driving a late model Corvette was rabbit hopping from one light to the next. After about the third time, he makes his jump and was a full car length ahead of me. I down shifted, floored the accelerator, caught up to him and the front of the Mazda came abreast to his front wheel well. The driver was flabbergasted. He just knew some inexpensive, compact car couldn't keep up with his Corvette, let alone catch him, no way. At the next light, the driver looked over at me and gave me a challenge sign. I wasn't going to take the bait. I had shown him what the Mazda was capable of and I didn't want to cause an accident or get a ticket. However, as the light was about to turn green, I revved the engine. When we got the green light, I accelerated - up to the stated speed limit.

Occasionally my sister, Victoria, would borrow the Mazda. One night on her way home to Harbor City, with my niece Michelle, some guys in two other cars began stalking them. I must also say that the Mazda was not only quick, it was nimble, as a friend that owned a 914 Porsche would attest. Anyhow, the guys in the other two cars began trying to do a boxing maneuver, one in front the other behind. Not fully aware that the cars were working together, Victoria had not initially noticed the car in front until she accelerated and tried to go around the car. When she changed lanes, the car in front also changed lanes.

"Oh-Oh Michelle, I think these guys are trying to bother us. Just hold on." Victoria said.

Victoria saw a major intersection approaching. She changed from the right lane to the left lane and put her left turn signal on. The car in front saw her change lanes, saw the left turn signal and positioned his car to block her from turning left. Victoria turned right. Right was the direction she really wanted to go and put the "pedal to the metal." They were not going to catch this Mazda

Estimating & Pricing

Eventually my performance at work got noticed by a manager, Lee, of Estimating & Pricing. He made a nice offer, to include a promotion to come work with him. It was in another building but with the same division. Even after a year, I would have gone to the new division if offered. But once again, due to my finance and Industrial Engineering background, I was asked to participate in something that was not in my job description. They wanted me to participate on the negotiation team. The negotiations would take place on the phone with the various contracting officers of the Army, Navy, and Air Force, operating out of Washington D.C. For the first four or five calls, I would listen in to hear the conversation, understand the protocols and get the tone of the negotiations. I was to say nothing, just sit and listen. On my first negotiations, we called the Customer, and four of us sat around the speakerphone. During the whole discussion, I said nothing until it got close to settling and coming to an agreement. We wanted to caucus to discuss our position and where we thought we could land.

Our guys would say that they wanted to "turn down" the speakerphone so that we could discuss things in private and where the party on the other end could not hear. Once that was done, I was free to speak. I pointed out some things where I believed the Navy was wrong in their logic and suggested that we not go below a certain number. It was a little higher than what they would have settled on, but I believed we could justify the numbers. We turned the speakerphone back on and the guys continued the negotiations. This process continued for about three months until one day I was in the conference room and a telephone repairman was there working. Out of curiosity, and for something that I had always been uncomfortable with, I needed assurance that "turning down" the speakerphone turned down communication both ways, our side and their side.

"Hi, my name is Mel, and I have a question to ask you."

"Hi Mel, I'm Steve. What can I do for you?

"Occasionally we will use this room for discussions with other groups. I was wondering about the volume control on the speakerphone. When you turn down the volume, does it turn it down for both parties?"

"No, it only turns down the volume of the speaker, not the microphone. The microphone stays active. The only way to deactivate the microphone is to put the other party on 'hold.' Otherwise, the party on the other end can hear just fine." The repairman said.

I thought, oh my lord, all these months, all those negotiations, and the person on the other end was able to hear us when we were discussing our strategy, saying what our acceptable numbers were, and what our drop-dead figures were. They could hear everything. And no one on the other end had enough integrity to tell us.

I immediately called the team together and informed them of my findings. We then began to develop a strategy to use this awareness to our favor. All is fair in love and war. We would "turn down" the speakerphone as always, this time however, we would have already outlined our strategy and talk about bogus numbers out loud. We would argue the same as always, talk about the Contract Administrator on the other end, as always, and reluctantly accept our bottom-line number, as always. Except, now, it was not our bottom-line number, close, but not bottom line. They thought it was and that was all we wanted. The Government people never did confess their awareness of our discussions. The way the charade ended, was a move to another conference room and a new phone. With the new phone, that operated differently, we would actually put the person on "hold" giving us the privacy we needed.

I'm sure the Government personnel were very disappointed that we changed our conference room.

Coaching Pop Warner Football

A friend of mine, Ben, worked in Hughes Procurement and was a Pop Warner football coach in the city of Carson, about 10 miles south of LA, and about 15 miles from where Gil and I lived. The team was called, "Carson Ravens." Ben asked if Gil and I wanted to help him coach. He would coach offense; Gil and I would coach defense. I took on the role of physical conditioning coach and would perform the exercises and run laps with the kids. By exercising with them, I could tell how much I was working them, and also embarrass them a little, in that they couldn't keep up with the "Old Man." I was 24 at the time. When you are 12 and 13 years old, anyone over the age of 20 is old. I knew that was how they thought and tried to play it to my advantage. Ben ran a very complex offense; one that I thought was too complicated for kids. It became very apparent in the games we played. We didn't win a game that season, but no team scored more than 14 points on us even though our offense was not on the field for very long. Our defense was on the field so often, as the offense would go three and out, that the kids that played defense just got tired. It was then that the opposing team would score, when our kids could hardly walk.

The following season, Ben could not coach, and asked if Gil and I would take over the team. I spoke to Gil and said that I can handle the offense and the kids, you take the defense and the moms. We became co-head coach of the team. We had a couple of kids returning, who warned the new-comers of my propensity to do heavy physical training (PT). As the training season began, we were still running laps, doing drills and other conditioning exercises when the other age groups were starting to put on their pads and having contact.

Our kids started to complain, so much so that the parents got involved. Gil and I discussed how we were going to handle the discontent.

I said to Gil, "I'll speak with the parents this one time, you take it back hereafter."

One evening, after practice, we called all the parents together.

I went over what our philosophy was.

"I told them, "We are not in the process of preparing for the game of football, we are in the process of preparing your kids for the game of life. Gil and I are about building character. We are on your side; and you should be on ours. After all, we have something that your kids want, game time. If your kid is not doing his homework, let us know. If your kid is not cleaning his room, let us know. If your kid is not being respectful, let us know. We will help you in changing that behavior by determining if he will start a game or how much he plays in a game. As far as physical training is concerned, here again, we have your child's well being in mind. Most kids that show up for football are not ready to take the punishment of football. Our job is to make sure your kids are ready for that punishment. The better fit they are physically, the less likely they will be to get hurt. Gil and I don't have any kids, so we are not here because we have a son playing; we are here because we care. Gil and I are here voluntarily; we aren't getting paid. Your kids are here voluntarily. You have a choice. You can have your child stay with the program, develop physical strength and strength of character or you can withdraw him from the program. That choice is yours."

With that said, I turned to Gil, in a voice that was loud enough for the parents to hear.

"Well Gil, I guess we'll know tomorrow if we have enough kids to make a team."

I walked away and left Gil with the parents. For practice the next day, I was pleased to see that not one parent pulled their child off the team. From that day forward, the support we got from the parents continued to increase.

Our first game was really big for us. Just coming off of a "no-win" season, there were a lot of unknowns. Gil and I were confident in the condition of our kids. Besides being in great physical condition, I was confident in their ability to execute the offense, he the defense. When the final seconds ticked off the clock, we not only won the game by 21 points, it was a shut out. The parents of course were elated. They saw the results of our program. The next game was going to be against last year's championship team, the Inglewood Sentinels. The game would be played on their home field. This would be the real test for our football squad. Miracles do happen. We won the game 14 – 7. We went on from there and won game after game. We had to play the Sentinels a second time, we lost 7 – 14. However, we and the Sentinels won our respective divisions with a one loss over-all record. If we were going to see each other again, both of us would have to win two playoff games and our respective divisions.

As fate would have it, there would be a third and deciding game between us and the Sentinels, the Championship. The Championship was held on a neutral field in San Pedro. This city is also a suburb of L.A. and is near the ocean. I mention this little fact, about being near the ocean, because as both of our teams marched out on the field, a low fog, just about ankle high, rolled in. It was eerie. It added another dimension to the game and somehow seemed fitting. We were down 14 – 0 at half time, but just before the break, we felt a shift in momentum. We knew we were going to come back in the second half. Knowing that, we asked the referees what method they will use for a tie breaker.

"We will use the college rule for a tie breaker." The referee said.

"The ball would be placed at the 20-yard line and each team would get four downs to score. At the end of the series, and no score, then the ball would be moved to the 50-yard line, and each team given four more downs. At the end of both series, which ever team has advanced the ball to the other side of the 50 wins."

We were OK with that.

We scored seven points in the third quarter and seven points in the fourth quarter. Game is tied. We played the whole game without our star running back Sam. He hurt is ankle the last game we played. His ankle was still swollen so I wouldn't put him in. At half time, many of the parents complained, but I reminded them, the safety and future of the kids was our greatest concern. Gil stood with me. We wanted to win, especially against Inglewood. However, win or lose, we had the best season Carson had ever had, and the kids played like champions. Sam, as it turns out, later got a full scholarship to Oklahoma, started for three years and ended up getting drafted by the Miami Dolphins. Who knows what would have happened had he played for us that night and really tore up his ankle? We didn't know the future, but we knew Sam had talent, and was really good.

In the fourth quarter, Inglewood began resorting to passing to try to win the game. I asked Gil to have alphabet to go all out to get a sack. Alphabet was Samoan and had a last name that seemed to have every letter in the alphabet and that none of us could pronounce, so we called him alphabet. He was medium height, stocky and strong. We put him in at nose tackle and just said, "Sick 'em." He was like a bulldog. From that point on they never threatened to score again. The game ended, 14 – 14. Overtime.

To our utterly and stark disappointment, the referees changed the tie-breaking method. Instead of each team having a series of four plays, we would have to alternate having possession after each play. This was a disadvantage to our offense. We often use one play to set up the next. By alternating possession, we would not gain that benefit. By now, the fog was knee-high and wispy. The hype before the game, the best two teams, the only loss was to each other, made the game electric from the opening kick-off. The fog only intensified what was already a thriller. When the referee placed the ball on the 50-yard line, because of the fog, the ball literally disappeared. This was going to be an interesting series of eight plays.

We had the ball first. I was extremely tempted to put Sam in. We had a play designed just for him. It was a pass play. We fake a tailback dive to Sam, he penetrates the line and is hit with the ball on a curling pattern about 10 yards beyond the line of scrimmage. We tried running it earlier in the game, but Sam's replacement didn't have the hands. Twice, the ball was there but he couldn't hang on. Gil came up to me and just said one word.

"Sam?"

"Tempted, but no," I said.

Gil looked at me, and then he said, "You're right, it's not worth it."

Inglewood tried a couple of unsuccessful pass plays. On the third play, we moved the ball about five yards on their side of the 50. On their third, they moved it back four and a half yards. The ball still on their side of the 50 for about a half yard. Our fourth and last play, we moved the ball another half yard. One yard on their side of the 50. The teams lined up. The fog swirling. A long count. Smart. A penalty now would give them the game. But our kids were well disciplined. They held back until the ball was snapped. The movement of 22 bodies kicked up the fog so that, from the sidelines, we could see very little. The referees rushed in to determine the placement of the ball. They started peeling bodies off of the pile. About ¾ of the football, or about eight inches, was on our side of the 50-yard line. They were awarded one point and thus won the game. We had played three games against each other, and in the end, there was only a one-point difference in the combined score. Comparing to what we did last year, a no-win season, we believed we had accomplished a phenomenal feat. It was almost a Cinderella story; we got invited to the ball but didn't get to kiss the prince. Gill and I coached for five more seasons, for a total of seven years. We actually announced that the sixth year was going to be our last, until something happened that encouraged us to coach for one additional year.

After the second year, the year we played for the championship, Gil and I were asked by the Inglewood coaching staff to coach for the city of Inglewood. The field was only two miles from where we lived, so the driving time was considerably reduced. There was nothing keeping us in Carson, as I mentioned earlier, neither of us had a son nor a relative playing on the team. We accepted the offer to coach in Inglewood. I think one of the motivations for the coaching staff of Inglewood to ask Gil and I to come join them was, it was a good way to eliminate one of your strongest competitors. Since, when we were at Carson, Inglewood Sentinels was the team we played for the championship last year.

At the beginning of our sixth year of coaching, we had a good group of kids. We had made the playoffs for four years running and this group looked like we would continue that string. As usual, in the beginning part of training, we would have, what is called, "full speed scrimmages." The kids would be in full pads, and we would run the offense against the defense, just as if it was a game. One player, John, who was a fullback on last year's team with another coach, was playing right guard for me this year. Neither he nor his dad was too happy about this fact. One evening after practice, John's dad came up to speak with me.

"Hey coach, I would like to speak with you." John's dad said.

"Sure," I said.

"Last year my son was starting fullback and I'd like to know why he isn't playing that position this year?"

"I looked at your son's ability real hard, and there are several things that I noticed; he is fast, but not as fast as the two players I have in front of him; and, his skill level is not up to their level. Our offense needs a pulling guard that is quick. Your son can be that player for us. I guarantee you that if he plays the guard position well, he will be noticed by the defense and will be picked up by the coaching staff to also play defense. I can leave your son at the fullback position, but I cannot guarantee that he would see much playing time. However, at the guard position, he will start."

Things began to happen just as I predicted. John was such a terror at the pulling guard position that Gil, who coached the defense, came up to me.

"Who is that kid? Where did you find him?" Gil said.

"You're only asking because you want him on defense."

"Mel, you know me too well."

"You can have him for half the practice."

"Thanks buddy, I'm glad you saw it my way" Gil said jokingly as he walked away.

The story doesn't end there but is in conjunction with another incident. That story follows.

That same year, Nathan, one of two halfbacks that were starting for us had a really bad attitude. In one game, where we were winning 48 – 0, in the third quarter, I started pulling out our starters. He came off the field complaining about being pulled from the game and that he wanted to set a record in yardage gained. He also wanted to run up the score since several kids on the other team went to the same school as he and he wanted "bragging rights." It was one of the few times, if not the only time, that I lost my cool. My action, so uncharacteristic, was so startling to the players and coaches that there was a momentary pause of action all along the bench. For that brief moment, everyone was focused on me rather than the game. As quickly as it happened, it just as quickly passed. I took control of my emotions and the situation and, in spite of Nathan's protest, I began making substitutions.

After the game, I met Nathan's parents and told them I would like to come to their house tomorrow, Sunday, to see Nathan. Sunday, I picked Nathan up from his home and took him to the park. We sat down on the grass and I just started speaking to him.

"Nathan, you are an extremely gifted athlete. There are a lot of things you do that you take for granted and that many kids your age cannot do. Unfortunately, there are some characteristics that you have acquired that are unbecoming. You have a lot of energy but you're lazy, always looking for the easy way out. You are a leader, but a clown. Because of your talent, many of the other kids look up to you, problem is you don't take things seriously. You always try to make a joke out of something or someone. At times, you can be an encourager, but selfish."

For two hours, I talked. He listened. At the end, I told him that if I saw a marked improvement in his attitude, performance, and behavior, that I would recommend that he be co-captain of the team and give him more game time. If he changed for the better, he would have earned both promises. I took Nathan home and thanked his parents for letting me have the time. The following week at practice, the change in Nathan was remarkable. He began hustling, encouraging others to hustle, and quickly became one of the recognized leaders. I kept my word, as he was rewarded by being named co-captain of the team.

At the end of the year, at the banquet luncheon, we were handing out trophies to the kids. Our team was called "The Warriors." Bruce, my converted fullback who played pulling guard and defense for us received our highest award and was presented with the "Mr. Warrior" trophy. Usually this award would go to a running back or quarterback position. This was the first time a lineman had ever received the award. Nathan received the second most coveted trophy, Most Valuable Player.

Gil and I were saying our good byes, since this was our last season coaching, when Bruce's Dad came up to us.

"I doubted you guys at first, but over time, I did see that you guys had my son's interest at heart. And for him to win that award, I can only say thank you." Bruce's dad said.

Wow. That really touched Gil and I, but it didn't change our decision to coach again. Nathan's mom and dad did. Right after Bruce's dad made his comment, Nathan's mom and dad approached Gil and I.

Nathan's mom said, "Mel, we don't know what you said to Nathan that Sunday you took him to the park, but he was a changed person when he returned. You took one boy away and brought us back another. Nathan began to settle down in school, he began being more mindful at home, the change was just unbelievable. His father and I just can't thank you enough."

His dad said, "I purposely came to a couple of practices and saw how you guys worked with him on the team, and how you continued to encourage him. It was remarkable. If for no other purpose than to give us a son, I'm glad Nathan had you guys as coaches."

With that, Gil and I looked at each other, and without speaking a word, agreed to coach for one more year.

As hard as I was on the kids, I was the disciplinarian and physical conditioning coach, every player new that if something happened to them in a game, they had my undivided attention. I would be the first on the field if they were hurt. I would walk off the field with them if they could, and if they needed more attention on the bench, I would be there. Although I did the play calling, if a player was hurt, I relegated that duty to an assistant or Gil would take over. I tended to the needs of the hurt player. I wanted the kids to know, they were more important to me, and Gil, than winning a game. I think they got the message.

More often than not, they would be the one to say, "I'm alright coach, the team needs you."

Although I have never seen any of the players after they left the team, Gil has encountered many of them. Occasionally when I see Gil, he would tell me, I ran into so and so and they said, "What's coach King doing these days, tell him I said Hi."

Then Gil would tell me they would always talk about the physical conditioning drills and running that I would have them do. They wondered how that "old man" could run so much and keep up with them doing all that other stuff. But they all said they were better for it.

A Challenge

Renee and I dated off and on for a couple of years before the dating became more frequent and more on the steady side. There were several times when certain things happened that almost brought our relationship to a halt. One incident was our first ski trip together. From our first date and continuing, I always treated Renee like a lady, opening doors for her, having an umbrella ready for her when it rained, and other things to make her feel special. Not so on the slopes. After we went through the equipment line and Renee got her skis, boots and poles, I showed her how they are arranged for easy carry. She halfway paid attention.

Once I arranged them, I then said to her, "OK, you can pick them up now."

"What, you mean you are not going to carry them for me?" She said.

"No. On the slopes, every person has to learn to take care of themselves. This is your first lesson, carrying your own equipment," I said.

"Mumble, mumble."

We got to an area where I thought would be a good place for Renee to put on her skis. She had her boots on and complained the whole time.

"I feel like Frankenstein in these things. How do they expect a person to walk? And besides, this is very un-lady like." Renee said.

She put on her skis, slid a little way and fell. She looked up at me, held her hand out for me to take it. I looked at her hand, looked her in the eyes, and shook my head.

"You do this on your own. I will tell you how, but you have to learn how to get up on your own."

"Mumble, mumble."

It took Renee about five minutes until she was standing again. To help keep her from falling so much, I showed her how to position her poles for support and balance. In her attempt to position her poles, she lost focus and; she did a slow-motion descent. When she hit the snow, I gave her a few seconds to gain her composure before challenging her to stand up again.

"Ok, think like a baby, they don't stop trying to walk just because they fall a couple of times."

She stood up and we slowly made our way to the bunny slope. I did capitulate and held on to her as we got onto the chairlift.

On the way up the hill, Renee looked down and said, "I have to come down that slope?"

"No problem, a piece of cake," I said.

As we were riding the chairlift, I walked Renee through the steps on how to exit the chairlift about a dozen times before we got to the end. The first few steps she executed flawlessly. She was doing good until about midway through the process. Slow motion descent. She was laying there in the snow, actually looking pretty good. I got her one of those nice looking "bunny suits" and it fitted her really nice. I was admiring her form when she instinctively reached out her hand again. I looked at her hand, looked her in the eye, and shook my head.

"Mumble, mumble. What happened to that Mel that I used to know? You're being so mean. I never thought I would ever get treated like this from you."

With that, tears began to form. Oh no, not tears. The bane of every guy, a women's tears. She almost had me. I was resolved not to give in. To add insult to injury, I pulled her to one side, to clear the landing from the chairlift. She didn't like being dragged. I really didn't drag her, I lifted her up from the back, under her arms, then I "pulled" her. She says "dragged." Once out of the way, I waited for her to stand up. This took another five minutes, because now we were on an incline; whereas before it was fairly level. The whole morning went like this, Renee sliding, her falling and getting up, about three hours worth. Close to the end of the third hour she was skiing half way down the bunny slope before she fell. Her time from snow to standing also improved. We broke for lunch.

The whole lunch time, Renee was on my case about being so mean and uncaring, and that she didn't like skiing. When she finished her quiet tirade, I told her she didn't have to come skiing with me in the future. However, I did remind her that Larry and I would go skiing with the ski club within the next few weeks. I didn't say it; I didn't think I had to. The ski club was co-ed with a lot of single ladies going on the trip. She could stay home, or she could come and watch over her investment. The choice was hers. We sat in the lodge for about an hour, about 30 minutes longer than I would have if I was by myself.

At the end of the hour I said, "OK, time to get back on the trail."

Renee just sat there.

"I don't want to go."

"You will be surprised how much you have learned. Before this day is up, you'll be coming down the hill without falling once. If you don't go now, you will never go again. And besides, you won't find a better instructor."

"I bet I can find a nicer one." Renee retorted.

With that we both laughed and I took her arm and Frankenstein and

Frankenstein's bride walked out of the lodge. This ski trip was a changing point in our relationship. Renee was challenged by seeing another part of me that she had never experienced before. What she didn't realize at the time was that I was developing her to be independent and more confident on the snow. I wasn't always going to be around, so she needed to be able to fend for herself. Skiing is a very personal sport, and confidence peppered with humbleness is the best mix. It wasn't fun for her at first, but it was best for her. I think at one time she called me "Coach King." For me, by my investment in time and energy, I was essentially letting her know that I was not interested in meeting somebody else while skiing or on a ski trip. I was making a commitment to her, if she was willing to accompany me on the next ski trip.

Back in the Office

At Hughes, negotiations were going well, and much improved since we made the change in telephones. One day the department manager, Lee, came to me and said that the company was having difficulty in negotiations on a major contract, the F-18 Radar. There were several clauses in the contract, one being an Economic Price Adjustment (EPA), that had multiple factors that were interrelated, and no one on the team was able to come up with a resolution. Lee was aware of my schooling; that I had both economics and math classes, and he thought that my background would be helpful in working the problem. He brought me on the team. For three days, I read and re-read the contract and the various clauses until a glimmer of an idea began to form. A matrix. There were many areas where the price of a component or subassembly were dependent upon successful completion of another component or subassembly. Added to the mix was a time factor that also impacted the price. I worked up a sample spreadsheet and gave it to Lee.

(As you read this you may say "OK, not so tough." Try doing it without the computers that we have on our desktops today.) This was done the old fashion way, hand written spreadsheets and a calculator. I don't recall how long it took for me to develop and complete the work, however, I do recall of many early mornings and late nights. I also recall that as the days passed, Lee began to hover over me as a hen would her chicks. This increased in frequency as the dead-line approached. As I completed a section, I would turn it over to the rest of the team so that they could write the intro, body and ending paragraphs. The morning of the day prior to submittal, I completed my work. The rest of the team spent the whole day and until about 10:00 PM that night to finish the proposal. We submitted it the next day. We were in competition with several other companies, one being Raytheon. It would be a month before we would know who the winner was. Lee called me into his office.

"Mel, I want to thank you for the work, the effort, and creative idea that you did on that F-18 proposal. When I showed them the first draft of what you did they were like, 'Why didn't I think of that?' The idea of a matrix, some parts three dimensional, was just, well great. I really feel good about the proposal we submitted. But to your credit, you thought of a solution to a problem that had all of us puzzled and hung in there with us until the end. Really, really proud to have you as part of my organization." Lee said.

It was about two months later that the winner of the F-18 Radar was announced, Hughes. You would have thought that something would have been done in recognition of my contribution in developing the winning proposal. Nothing was ever said or done. Our department was in a support role; however, our contribution was extremely significant. Lee did apologize for the company, he also believed some recognition should have been forthcoming, and said that he personally would try to make it up to me. "Civilians don't often appreciate nor reward leadership, innovation, or dedication." (Gen Olds, Commandant of Cadets, U.S. Air Academy) But I know, being "Black can make a difference."

Musing Thought

Many times, in my career I have heard that companies often look but cannot find capable, educated, and "articulate" Black individuals. Whenever I heard that, I would say "Here am I." However, I could never really believe that a search was conducted in earnest. Too many times my performance was demonstrably better than my peers (members of the Good ole Boys), yet many times I saw where they were rewarded for much less. Another thing. Ever notice how "Articulate" is often used when describing a Black person but not necessarily so for other nationalities? It's as if being capable of speech is rare for a Black person. Frequently its use is intended to be a compliment; however, to me, it has the opposite effect, and unfortunately, I heard it used to describe me way too often.

Life Changing Events

My Sister Vic, was a church goer. She sang in the choir at the church where her father-in-law was a Baptist preacher. She would attend this church every Sunday; and if not that church, she would find another Baptist church to attend. She would even listen to church music on the radio when it was played on Sundays. She was really religious. One day she was told about this church which was pastured by a young and dynamic pastor that supposedly had a different way of imparting the bible. The church was in Inglewood and was called Crenshaw Christian Center. She was told that there were a lot of young people coming and they were carrying their bibles with them. Vic went to the church to visit. After her first time going, she knew she had to make this her new church home. Her dilemma was, how does she tell her father-in-law and husband that she wanted to make a change.

She worked it out. After about three months she began telling me about the church and that I should come. It wasn't working, so she changed her tactics and began talking to Renee. Renee was raised catholic, so what Vic was saying was a little bit of a stretch for Renee. Vic convinced Renee to visit the church, so Renee asked if I would accompany her. One Sunday, Vic, Renee and I went to the church. The auditorium sat about 1200 people and it was about two-thirds full. The music was much better than what I was used to at a Baptist church. The choir actually sang in harmony and the instruments were tuned. The pastor, Fred Price, came out and essentially taught a lesson, using the bible as his reference book. Very unusual, and very interesting. I only went that one Sunday.

A couple of weeks later, one of my friends, Nate, was over and Renee happened to stop by. We were sitting around talking when Renee brought up the subject of attending church.

"Nate, why don't you go to church with me some Sunday, or to a Tuesday night Bible Study?"

Nate, knowing my background, spoke out and said, "I'll go to church when Mel goes to church."

"Well, I guess you're going; cause Mel already has." Renee said.

Nate looked like he had been hit with a sack of sugar. He looked at me with incredulity.

He said, "How could you, I trusted you."

We all committed to go back to church for Tuesday Night Bible Study. At the end of the study that Tuesday night, Pastor Fred gave, what is called, an "Altar Call." This is an invite to accept Jesus Christ into your life as your Lord and Savior.

Prior to giving the invitation, Pastor Fred would say "Every head bowed and every eye closed."

Then he would say, "If you would like to accept Jesus Christ as you Lord and Savior, raise your hand. Or if you want to make this your church home, raise your hand. If you responded to either invitation, leave your seat and make your way down the aisle to front."

Nate was sitting on the other side of Renee, so imagine my surprise when Nate excused himself to get by. I didn't know that he responded to the invitations.

Nate began changing from that night onward.

A month or so later I began to go to the church but would attend bible study prior to the church service. Pastor Billy Ingram, a young pastor our age, was teaching. I had a lot of questions. Sometime during this enlightenment, I realized that I needed to change and accept Jesus Christ as my Lord and Savior as well. My relationship with Renee also changed. It wasn't too long thereafter that I asked Renee to marry me; and, I asked Pastor Billy if he would conduct the ceremony.

In beloved memory of Dr. Billy Ingram, always a friend.

A Wedding

Since my dad died and was not around when I was young, I did not have a mentor to guide me in etiquette and art of making a proposal. I made a Faux Pas that really upset Renee's dad, my future father-in-law. I didn't go to him first, to request Renee's hand in marriage, before I proposed to her. As a result, he said that he was not going to pay for the wedding. My initial response, which fortunately I didn't say out loud was, "Fine, won't send you an invitation." If he wasn't going to pay for the wedding, then he didn't earn the right to walk her down the aisle or "give her away." Nowadays, Renee often reminds me how stubborn I used to be. What I thought about saying to her dad, I so much as said this to Renee. I was already paying for our Honeymoon, her car, her credit cards, and now this. One Sunday, shortly thereafter, as God often orchestrates, Pastor Billy and Fred taught on Forgiveness. I didn't want to hear it. I sat through Bible Study and the church service with forgiveness ringing in my ears but hardness in my heart. Then I had enough nerve to argue with God.

"Why should he be permitted to walk her down the aisle? He wants his cake and eat it too. He ain't contributing, so why should he get the benefit. Everybody will think that he's paying for the wedding."

Then I heard in my spirit, "Why should you have the benefit of eternal salvation when you ain't paid nothing, my Son did?"

"Ouch." That was the beginning of my arguments with God. By the way, I have lost every one. Renee's dad walked her down the aisle.

Renee and I got married at Yamashiro's, a Japanese restaurant in Hollywood, on 8 April 1978. The restaurant had a screen covered atrium whose garden was fashioned after the most beautiful gardens of Japan. It had a variety of colors, a flowing stream with large carp, and a bridge that crossed over the stream unto a walkway that meandered through the garden.

About four steps lead down into the garden. The ceremony was to take place just at the base of the stairs. The garden itself was rectangular shaped and the dinning tables and chairs that were placed around the sides were elevated and looked down into the garden. This elevated position is where our guest sat. We had the reception in an adjacent ballroom.

It had been raining all that Saturday, which was very unusual in LA for the month of April. Many of our friends asked what we were going to do, since the wedding was essentially outside. The guest tables and chairs were under cover, but the screen was the only thing that covered the garden area. Renee's and my response were that we have faith that the weather would clear and the wedding would go on as planned. We made no alternate plans. We were trusting God. It was a late afternoon wedding, and as the time approached, it continued to rain.

I was in a side room when one of the groomsmen came to me and said, "The valet parking is having difficulty parking all of the cars, only about half of your guest are in the building. There is a long line of cars still trying to come up the hill. It may take another half hour before all the guests arrive. What do you want to do?"

Without hesitation, I looked at Pastor Billy, who was sitting with me, and I said, "Pastor, Billy, please make an announcement to the guest that are seated, that we have taxed the valet services of the restaurant and that we will have about a 30-minute delay."

About 300 people were in attendance. Although the restaurant knew the number, I'm sure the valet folks were not prepared. During that half hour delay, the rains stopped and the late afternoon sun came out. When the late sun came out, it cast a golden glow upon the garden. It was surreal. As beautiful as the garden was by itself, it was as if God was saying, "You ain't seen nothing yet." He added the finishing touch. My sister Victoria and a friend of ours, Charles, both sang individually, and then a duet. During the course of our saying our wedding vows, we asked Pastor Billy to take advantage of a captured audience and talk about our Lord and Savior, Jesus Christ, and what he means to Renee and I. Of course, I am biased, but many people said it was the most beautiful wedding they had ever attended.

The next day, Renee and I flew to Hawaii. We landed on Oahu, spent four days there and then flew to Maui for three more days.

The Honeymoon - Hawaii

We had a commanding room of Honolulu and the ocean from the balcony of our hotel room. On Oahu, we did a lot of the tourist things. The first day we got on a tour bus to tour the island. We saw the last of the few pineapple fields remaining and asked about the sugar cane. Property was becoming so valuable in Hawaii that the farming industry was disappearing and being replaced by tourism. On the tour, we saw several places we wanted to visit. The Polynesian Cultural Center, Hannauma Bay, a Luau, and a dinner cruise around the island. That night we went to the Luau. They cooked a whole pig right on the beach as done according to Hawaiian culture. It was fabulous.

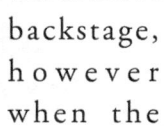

While at the Luau we saw a show where the audience was invited (ladies only) to participate. At first, they were taking volunteers. Renee, of course, as shy as she is, did not raise her hand nor anything else that might imply she was interested. Didn't matter, attendants from the show came into the audience to encourage the "reluctant ones." They took the ladies backstage where, Renee later told me, they showed them a few local dance moves. Renee said she made sure she was in the back. She may have been in the back, backstage, however when the curtain came open, there she was, front and center. Her embarrassment was obvious and I couldn't stop laughing. On our honeymoon and already Renee wanted to put me in the dog house.

The next day we went to Hanauma Bay for snorkeling. The water was so clear it was remarkable. Renee doesn't swim, so it took some convincing to get her in the water. She stayed in water that was just above her waist. I went out about 50 – 75 yards, just before the reef. Fish of multiple color and size were everywhere. It was very serene and peaceful. As I was coming back to the beach, all of a sudden, the fish, as one, all started swimming toward the beach. My first thought, JAWS. I quickly turned around to see what was coming and was relieved to not see a dorsal fin. The reef acts as a barrier to large fish so I had felt relatively safe in swimming so far out from the beach. But when the fish reacted the way they did, I knew for sure I was in trouble. As I continued to swim toward the beach, I discovered what caused the fish to react the way they did. Several snorkelers were throwing out bread. The fish near me were over a hundred yards from where they were throwing out bread; yet, the fish were able to detect this and swarmed the area. Amazing.

The following day we went to the Polynesian Cultural Center. We had a rental car and took the long way to get to the center. We wanted to look at a few other sites and see Hawaii up close and personal. It took a whole day and was extremely entertaining. While there we tasted "Poi" a Hawaiian staple that is made from the Taro plant. The Wikipedia definition: Poi is a Hawaiian word for the primary Polynesian staple food made from the corn of the Taro plant (known in Hawaiian as kalo). Poi is produced by mashing the cooked corm (baked or steamed) until it is a highly viscous fluid. Water is added during mashing and again just before eating, to achieve a desired consistency, which can range from liquid to dough-like (poi can be known as two-finger or three-finger, alluding to how many fingers you would have to use to eat it, depending on its consistency). The stuff tasted awful. We had a choice to take a spoonful or a bowl. Renee and I both opted for the spoon. Glad we did.

While in Hawaii, we were told that everyone has to see the "Don Ho" show. So, we did. He put on a great show and got the audience involved. No, Renee didn't go on stage this time. While on Oahu, Renee made the comment about how strange is the name of the main highway.

"Where did they come up with the name 'Like-Like,' and I wonder what it means. Renee said.

Now we are on our Honeymoon, so I just looked at her and grinned.

"Well, what? Why are you grinning? What did I say that was so funny?" Renee asked.

"Wel-l-l-l, you said Like-Like, as in 'I like you' it's pronounced 'lee-kay, lee-kay.' But then again, you are not an islander," I said.

"And neither are you buddy. Just for that, I'm renting you a doghouse for sure tonight."

"Un-uh, doghouses are not allowed on Honeymoons."

After four days on Oahu, we went to the island of Maui. Maui was very quiet and not nearly as developed as Oahu. There we relaxed more on the beach and just chilled. As with most vacations, it was over way too quickly.

Vacation Opportunities

Renee and I were married four years before Aaron was born, on Father's Day, 21 June 1982. Prior to that time, we took full advantage of being "Home Alone" without any children. Often times we would take off for a weekend, load up our bikes, and go someplace that is within a four-hour drive. One such instance was to Newport Beach, California, about two hours south of Los Angeles.

One anniversary weekend, on a Saturday, we got up real early in the morning to catch a flight to San Francisco. As soon as we landed, we rented a car and drove to Seal Rocks, just south of San Francisco. This was our first stop of the day, and overlooking Seal Rocks is the Cliff House where they advertise having 1001 different kinds of omelets. The restaurant has undergone several changes throughout its history. It first existed as a hotel (picture 1), having a fantastic view of the Pacific Ocean and the seals that declared the nearby rock formation as home. Unfortunately, we never saw the hotel in this condition as it was destroyed by fire (picture 2) in 1907. What replaced the hotel was no-where near as grandeur, but was the facility (picture 3) we visited to have breakfast. The Cliff House of today (picture 4) is modern looking and much more upscale than the red colored, beachfront, overgrown stand that we visited that day.

From Seal Rocks and the Cliff House, we went into San Francisco and drove down Lombard St. known as the crookest street in the world. From Lombard St. we drove around San Fran to Telegraph Hill and Coit Tower. From there we drove down to cross the Golden Gate Bridge on over to Sausalito. We had lunch in Sausilito and strolled the water-front path by the rocks and marina. It was a typical California day, sun was out, gentle breeze, people wearing shorts, sunglasses and foot thongs. We found a nice shaddy place to relax, and wouldn't you know it, two hours went by (snap!) just like that.

We got the sand out of our eyes and went browsing in the nearby shops. Normally I don't do malls or browse, but on our anniversary and Renee's birthday, I acquiesce and keep a smile on my face. Renee knows this and takes full advantange. After going through shop after shop, we decided that we were going to go back to San Fran for dinner at Alioto's. Alioto's is a well known eatery, famous for its seafood and sceanic marina view. We found our way back to the car, went back over the Golden Gate Bridge, on to Alioto's. We had a very relaxing dinner comprised of lobster and King Crab legs. We watched the sun set behind the Golden Gate Bridge and the hills of Sausilito. It was gorgeous. I looked at my watch and notice that time was getting away. We had a plane to catch. We paid for our meal and reluctanly walked to the car and drove to the airport. We arrived back in Los Angeles late that same Saturday. As we drove home from the airport, we began reflecting on the day and all the things that we did. . . in one day. It was a great day, and to spend that kind of day with someone you love, couldn't be better.

Trip to Denver

One summer Renee and I went to see Rick and Doris. Rick was the captain that I befriended while at the Air Force Academy. We stayed in touch over the years and attended each other's wedding. Renee and I are known for getting people out of their comfort zone, so our visit with Rick and Doris would be no different. One of the first things we did was to organize a trip to a national park, just north of Fort Collins.

"Hey Rick, why don't you call some friends and let's go to a park and get some exercise," I said.

"What Park did you have in mind?" Rick Asked.

"The one just above Fort Collins. I hear they have good walking trails, and besides, the Aspen leaves should be full color 'bout now."

"OK, I'll make a few calls. I'll take off work and we can go tomorrow."

We made it to the park and made a day out of it. While at the park, and after a few hours on the trail, I overheard Rick and one of his friend's talking.

"Hey Rick, were do you know Mel and Renee from?"

"I knew Mel when he was at the Air Force Academy. He was a cadet and I was an instructor. He had been in the regular Air Force, was a little older than the other cadets and just had more experience in life; and it showed. We've stayed in touch ever since he got out of the Air Force."

"No wonder. A cadet huh? Boy, he and his wife sure got a lot of high energy. I live in Denver, high altitude an' all, and I'm huffing and puffing. They are from Los Angeles, and he and his wife look like they are out on a stroll. They ain't even breathing hard."

"Yeah, I know. Every time they come to Denver, we are always doing something involving or requiring some kinda athleticism. You should see them when they go skiing. Mel doesn't know how to come off the mountain. Renee will stop to have lunch, pulling Mel kicking and screamin' the whole time. They are a neat couple though."

The Aspen trees were in full color and was quite a treat for Renee and I. We were oohing and aaahing about the colors and contrast of colors between the Aspens and evergreens. Of course, Rick and the others, who see it every year, it was like, "Yeah, it's nice."

A couple of years later, we made it back to Denver to see Rick, Doris, and Dawn, their new baby girl.

Back at Work

When I returned from my honeymoon, my manager, Lee called me into his office.

Lee said, "Since you have gotten married, I know you are going to be needing extra money, so while you were gone, I was able to get you a raise. And besides, I told you I owe you for that F-18 job you did."

That raise was much appreciated. In my experience, Lee was an exception from all the managers in which I have had to work with. He recognized my work ethic, my talent and commitment to the company; and would often say so. In contrast to this, during this same time period, I had another experience that showed the selfishness of some managers. I was walking back to my desk from one of the other departments when I walked past an office where two managers were talking. Just as I passed the door, I heard my name being mentioned. I stopped, backed up and poked my head in the door and said,

"Did I just hear my name being mentioned?"

One of the managers looked at the other and said, "What are the odds of that happening?"

"Come on in Mel and have a seat. Before we say anything, you have to promise that you will not repeat this."

The mere fact that these managers were willing to trust me said a whole lot about my reputation within the company, even more so being Black.

"Whatever you say, I will not repeat it, nor will I take action if it is negative."

"Well Mel, we wanted you to come to our department and were willing to make you a supervisor to get you. But your Assistant Controller wouldn't let you go. He had some cock 'n bull story about your contribution to the department, that you didn't have supervisory experience, on and on. We argued with him and said that we were willing to take that chance. We lost the battle. We later found out that he has a grudge against you since you know his boss and have access to him. Bottom line is, he doesn't like you and we believe he is just jealous." One of the managers said.

Man, the things that you don't know.

"Don't know what I did to him. True, I do know his boss, Chuck, quite well. He knew of me within six months of my working at Hughes. I had another manager that didn't seem to like me. However, that got turned around, I got a promotion, and Chuck had to approve the added bonus I got."

"As we said the Assistant Controller's excuse was pretty lame."

"OK, thanks for being honest with me. I won't say anything. It will be hard, but I gave my word."

With heavy steps, I walked back to my desk. Another six months would pass before Lee was able to get me a promotion that was equivalent to a supervisor.

A New Project

Right after the promotion, I got a request to interview for the supervisor of a Project Control (PC) position on a new project, called "Roland." Roland was a twin missile platform, mounted on a tracked vehicle, that was anti-aircraft, anti-tank, and just about anti-anything. It was going to be the first, all metric program for Hughes. I won the position and was tasked to hire four additional people. I thought I was going to be able to recruit who I wanted. Didn't happen. I had my eyes on a couple of good people, just in case I ever got into a position to hire. I was given four individuals (no options) that had questionable performance in the department from which they were coming. I figured I could work with most people but I didn't like the fact that the deck was being stacked against me. However, I accepted the challenge.

Over the following months our organization blossomed into an organization that was enviable by most other supervisors. Every month we had to submit to Finance the actual hours and dollars spent on the project. This report was by subassembly by department. We consistently were the first to submit with the least number of errors. Once again, remember all this tabulation was done by hand and old fashion desktop calculators. Desktop computers and electronic spreadsheets still didn't exist. Whenever the four people in my department would meet people from other PC groups or Finance, and a discussion ensued, my team would always say how they enjoyed their job. They would talk about the cross training that goes on, that each would substitute for the other, that their boss (me) gave them an assignment and expected them to figure out how to make it happen, without telling them how to make it happen; and, the conversation would continue in this vein. This happened so often that I was asked to not have my team talk to the other PC groups, and even some of the people in Finance. My team was just enjoying their jobs too much.

Strange that none of the company managers ever came to me to ask how I managed to have such an efficient organization with people that other organizations didn't want.

Two of my team members, one a woman, and the other, a recent college graduate fought like they were sister and brother. One time they were in such a dog and cat fight, a manager passing by was seriously concerned.

"Mel, are you going to let them carry-on like that or are you going to intervene? He asked.

"Intervene in what?" I asked.

"That fight that is about to erupt. Sounds like they are about to tear each other's throat out."

"Oh, that, that happens all the time. Come back in five minutes, they'll be talking to each other in a way that you'll never knew that it happened."

The manager was shaking his head as he walked away. I knew my team and I knew they were developing passion about their work. That was why we had the fewest errors and best delivery. I wasn't about to change it. The height of wanting to suppress the enthusiasm of my team reached its apex one afternoon. My manager, Roger, called me into his office.

He said, "Mel I'm getting complaints that your people are laughing too much. I was asked to see if you could do something about it."

With that comment, I started laughing myself. "You mean you had a complaint about laughing? How hilarious; and, you want me to have them stop enjoying their job? Incredulous. You tell me what you would prefer. Right now, our group is the first into Finance with our numbers, and we have the least number of errors. On top of that, the program is being managed to where we are at or under budget in every category. Now, you tell me which you would prefer, laughter, or for us to begin failing in these other areas?"

Roger looked me in the eye, and for several seconds we locked eyes as if we were dueling. I didn't back down.

Finally, he said, "Just get out of here. I'll handle those other managers." Our department continued to be the rowdiest and best performers.

One-day Roger and I were called in to see the Program Director, Rudy, about a budget issue with one of the performing departments. The Director told us what the issue was and about his concern. After listening, I asked a few questions and then offered my suggestion. The Director liked what I said and asked if I wanted his assistance. I politely explained that I thought I could handle this myself but would keep him in reserve if things got out of hand. Shortly thereafter I was dismissed. Roger and the Director continued with the meeting. Later that day I saw Roger in his office.

Roger said, "Mel, when you left Rudy's office, Rudy and I had a short conversation about you. He really liked your idea, but when you left, he said 'Cocky S.O.B. isn't he?' He was a little put out that you believed that you didn't need his help."

"Roger, he is paying me to do what I do. I am proving that I know what I am doing. You have not had to intervene in any budget issues, why would I want to involve the Program Director?" I said.

Roger had no rebuttal.

I was on the program for about 10 months when I was asked to interview for a Section Head position in Estimating and Pricing for another division. My experience for this position was the job I had just prior to my current position, working with Lee. In fact, it would be Lee's equivalent position. I would be responsible for the group, about six people, that is developing the estimates and proposals for the whole division, comprised of about 3500 people. The division builds traveling wave tubes (TWT), gyrotrons, gigatrons and other products that powered radars. The division was located in the city of Lomita, south of LA and about 13 miles from my home. I interviewed with the controller, Dick, and assistant controller, Elliot at a restaurant, that lasted for about an hour and a half. A couple of weeks passed until the day Roger called me into his office.

"Mel, I got a call earlier today, Lomita wants you. It's a sad day for me, but I am happy for you."

Roger was Black and one of just a few Black Managers at Hughes. I will be going to a division of 3500 people and two black managers; I will make the third. Yes, this is in Southern California, circa 1978, the greater LA area.

"Mel, understand that, because you are Black, you will be going into a pack of wolves. You will have to establish yourself very quickly that you can run with them, hunt with them, and most importantly, fight along side of them, not against them. If you fight against them, remember, there are more of them than there are of you. It has not been easy for me, and it won't be easy for you. Every step you take, every move you make will be scrutinized and second guessed. Continue to be as confident in your decisions as you have been here. You have done a great job for me here and you are deserving of this opportunity." Roger said.

After leaving Roger's office, I stopped by to see Earl, the associate Program Manager. Earl and I got along extremely well and I didn't want to leave without saying good-bye. Neither of us knew at the time that destiny wasn't finished with us yet.

Accomplishments at Radar Systems Group

•Turned a costly waste product disposal into a money-making project through a gold recovery process, saving the company tens of thousands of dollars.

•Increased usefulness of Motion-Time-Measurement Studies from just manufacturing hour's determination to budget and cost analysis tool. Changed entire methodology of the way the Budget Control department determined manufacturing budgets and profits.

• Developed Cost Matrix that enabled Hughes to put together a winning bid for the F-18 radar contract

• Took over as lead negotiator for F-14 Contract even though I was not in the Contracts department. Profit margins on all contracts increased.

• Managed and coached a ragtag team of unwanted personnel into a coveted department, demonstrating "First in Class" for financial reporting, data keeping, and Budget Control.

A Bike, Rider, & Purse

One late afternoon on the way home, traveling through Westchester, (which is near the L.A. Airport), when I saw this lady run out of a store screaming;

"My purse! He stole my purse!"

From my vantage point (A) I saw a teenager on a bike with what looked like a purse dangling from his handlebars riding as fast as he could away from the store(dotted line). The streets were crowded so there was no way I could turn around in the car to head this person off. I pulled over, (A) got out of the car and ran around the block where I thought the person would pass (shortest route to B). Sure enough, just as I got to the corner, the guy on the bike also arrived (B). Without thought I tackled the guy and pulled him off his bike. We scuffled a few moments but I was able to get a Japanese hand-lock on him, got his arm behind his back and then got him to the ground. Once on the ground, I then put my knee in his back while still keeping him in the hand-lock. As I looked around to make sure he didn't have any accomplices, I saw two other guys, on bikes, across the parking lot, about 100 yards away (C). They were looking and pointing at us but were not coming in our direction. I made a mental note of their location.

"Let me go, I didn't do nothing," The guy said, while on his stomach.

"Do you always carry a purse?" I asked.

"Let me go. It's my sister's purse."

"Yeah, right. You're not going anywhere buddy so you may as well get comfortable."

It was a weekday, and there were a lot of people around. The crowd got bigger once it was obvious there wasn't going to be any additional violence happening. The lady whose purse was stolen was a long block away and had not yet shown up. I guess she gave up on getting her purse back, although she did see me getting out of the car and giving chase. It was a good five minutes before a security guard showed up and began asking questions.

"OK, what's happening. Who did what?" The security guard asked.

"I didn't do anything. This guy just came out of nowhere and jumped me."

I had a shirt and tie on. My suit coat was left in the car.

"Sure, I always dress up to go and tackle guys on a bike. I do it all the time," I said sarcastically.

"My purse. That's my purse." The lady finally shows up. And I must say, at the right time.

"Whoa, wait a minute. How do we know it's your purse?" The security guard asked.

"Well, I think that would be easy enough. Ask her, her name, address and see if it matches anything in the purse. Or describe what is in the purse," I said.

Up until now, I wouldn't let anyone touch the purse, not even the security guard.

"My name is Helen, and I live on …."

The security guard picked up the purse, checked the ID and confirmed that the purse belonged to Helen.

I looked at the security guard and noticed he had handcuffs.

"Hey, would you mind putting handcuffs on this guy so I can get up. And, I need to go move my car, I don't want it towed," I said.

By now I was running late to whatever meeting I was going to, so I gave Helen my business card.

"Here is my business card. If the police want a witness, have them call me and I will be in court with you to testify."

"I am so glad you got my purse back. I don't know how to thank you enough." The woman said.

"You are quite welcome ma'am."

I went back to my car. Oh boy, talk about illegal parking. I was on a corner, red lines, and next to a fire hydrant. The angels had my back. Praise the Lord.

Married, Plus a Couple of Years

One Saturday night, Renee and I were going to see Donna Summers, at the Universal Amphitheater, with a friend of ours John, and, Donna's sister Linda. Donna had just bought Linda a red Mustang, convertible with white top, so we were going to go out to celebrate. Just so happens that Donna was having a concert. Many people are probably not aware that the two backup singers for Donna are also her sisters. Linda has a fantastic voice and would do great as a backup singer as well; with one exception…see looked too much like Donna. The producers didn't want Linda to be a distraction from Donna, so Linda never got the opportunity to sing with her sisters. John and Linda came by our home to pick up Renee and I, we then headed to Hollywood.

I told John, "Wow, we're riding in a red convertible Mustang with the top down, a gorgeous smog-free LA day, and with two beautiful women. Life couldn't get any better than this!"

We laugh the whole time on the way to the concert.

As we got into Hollywood and had to stop at a few signal lights, people would point at Linda, and you could see the expression or curiosity on their faces, "Is that Donna Summers?" Linda of course would play it up, wave to folks and blow kisses. We approached the back lot of the Amphitheater where a security guard was stationed. He saw John, who was driving and asked for a parking pass.

He then looked over at Linda and said, "Oh, my apologies, Miss

Summers, we have a spot reserved for you, right this way."

We went to the assigned spot, got out and tipped the guard.

We had planned from the beginning to have dinner at the park, so we set out to find a place where we could sit down and have a quiet meal.

We went to this one restaurant and the hostess told us that "Because of the Donna Summers Concert, we are completely booked. There is about an hour wait."

However, the Maître D came up to the desk just as we were about to walk away.

He called out, "Miss Summers, just a moment. We are so glad that you were able to join us this evening, we have a table reserved for you."

We looked at the hostess and smiled, she mouthed "I didn't know."

The Maître D also looked at the hostess, but not with a smile.

"That's OK, daaarlin'." Linda replied.

The Maître D sat us at a booth that provided both privacy for us and publicity for the restaurant at the same time. It was like sitting in a bay window that jutted out a little from the restaurant. Because the booth was recessed, very little of our conversation could be heard. However, because it jutted out, we could be seen by passer-bys that went by on the walkways, an inexpensive advertisement for the restaurant.

As we sat there, out of the blue, Linda said, "Well, I'll give it 10 minutes."

"10 minutes for what?" I asked.

"10 minutes before someone becomes brave enough to ask for an autograph."

"Really? You think that will really happen?"

"Let's wait and see."

It was almost 15 minutes before the first person came. A young girl, asking to have Donna's autograph for her daddy. Before long, Linda had signed about eight pieces of paper; and, several more people were in line to get an autograph before the Maître D came, apologized profusely, and ushered everyone back to their seats. For the interruption by the other diners, dinner was on the house.

Donna puts on a fantastic concert. A friend of ours that Donna met at one of our bible studies led the dance troop. Dancing was a new addition for Donna and it really added life to the whole performance. We were glad to see our friend on stage and pleased to know that he would be on tour with her. After the concert, we went backstage. Donna, as usual, had an entourage following her so we couldn't get close to speak with her. Linda even tried to make eye contact with her sister to no avail. After that, John, Linda, Renee, and I went and found a table in a corner and continued with our own conversation and having fun doing it.

Every once in a while, we would get strange looks from some of the other people whenever we got too loud, laughing and everything. I'm sure they were wondering who we were, and how could we have so much fun without Donna. And I am absolutely sure that they began wondering even more so when Donna disengaged herself from her entourage and came and joined us at the table.

Donna sat with us for a short while and then said, "Well, I really would rather stay here with you guys, but duty calls." Donna got up and immediately was immersed by those that were waiting on her to join them. We finished out the evening with a leisurely walk back to the car. On the way home, we kept the top down on the Mustang and decided to drive down Hollywood Blvd. There were a lot of cruisers that night, so we had to drive really, really slow. Of course, the Hollywood set would have known that Donna Summers was in concert that night, and wow, there she goes in a red Mustang convertible. Linda waved and blew kisses up and down the boulevard. People on the sidewalk waved, those in their cars blew their horns. It was a fun night as we turned down La Brea to head home.

Section Head – A New Division

I reported in to work at the Lomita division; and, as is often the case, encountered a disgruntled employee, Bruce, who believed that he should have gotten the position that I now have. It took about three months, but one day Bruce came into my office and closed the door.

Bruce said, "I want to apologize for my behavior these past few months. I know that I was resentful of your coming on board and because of that, I didn't very much like you. It was only recently that I began to appreciate the changes that have been made, the respect the department is getting, and how you have been fair with me. Besides all that, it wasn't your decision to look outside the organization and not hire someone within the division. If I am to remain angry, I have been angry at the wrong person."

I said, "Bruce, thank you for saying what you just said. You see, I fully understood what you were going through and what you had to process. Now that I know there is no animosity, I want to ask you, do you mind being in charge if I go on vacation or if I am out of the office a few days?

"You mean you would trust me with that responsibility? Even after I have acted the way I have?" Bruce said.

"I never questioned your ability. Quite honestly, it was your attitude; and, I suspect that attitude may have been the reason why you didn't get this position. What I want to do now, if you don't mind my coaching you, is put you in a position where you can be noticed and get that promotion."

"I don't think I have ever had anyone so honest with me before. You would really do that?"

"My next time away from the office, I will send out a memo stating that you are in charge while I am away. That memo will be in effect until I send out something different."

It was nice to know that I had won Bruce over and made him a convert. The thing that I believe that was contributing to the department's growing respect within the company was the "homework" that I implemented. Before any pricing or estimating meeting, everyone, including myself, in the group had to research the cost, quantity, profit, contract terms & condition, etc. of several prior contracts before going to the meeting. In this way, we became a valuable reference and resource tool. Previously, the guys went to proposal meetings sat along the sidelines and just took notes or directions that were dictated to them. Now, they were being asked, "What did we sell those for before? Was there a quantity discount? Who did we sell them to? How long was the contract? When did we sell them?"

We became an integral part of the meetings, and if we weren't informed of a meeting, oftentimes they wouldn't start the meeting until someone would come and get us.

It was about eight to nine months later when Bruce came into my office and said that he got an offer at another division, and it was a promotion.

I was at this division for about a year when I received my MBA in Management/ Finance. Hughes was a great company in encouraging continuing education. I had full re-imbursement, as long as I had a "C" or better in my classes. As I reflect back over that time period, I am at a lost as to how I accomplished the things I did within a 24-hour period. I had a full-time job, carried a full load (12 units) at night school, coached Pop Warner football; worked on my thesis, and, during this time period, I got married. Moreover, I graduated Suma Cum Laude from Loyola Marymount (all "A"s and one "B") for my graduate work. My thesis is a story in itself.

The Thesis

While working at the El Segundo division, I met a gentleman, whose name happens to be Mel, selling custom car mats as a side business. People would come to him; place their order and he would bring back their mats within a two-week period. I watched Mel, how he was going about conducting his business, and determined that he would be a good candidate business for my thesis. I approached Mel about my idea and asked if he would permit me to work alongside of him. He would get counsel, free of charge, I would get my thesis. A fair trade.

Once I got Mel's agreement to work together, I had to get the professor, Mr. Scott, at school to approve the topic of my thesis. I met with Mr. Scott earlier to inform him that I wanted to work with a start-up company that made car and truck floor mats. He was not very much in favor of the project and questioned who would want custom car mats? I told him I thought it would be good for me since it would be a start-up company and, because of that, there were a lot of things that I would have to do, more so, than if it was an established enterprise. One day following the meeting with Mr. Scott, I asked Mel to make up a set of black car mats with yellow print, using the most sophisticated design we had. Mr. Scott's car was yellow. My next meeting with Mr. Scott was in two weeks.

Two weeks later, I walked into Mr. Scott's office, a package in hand.
"Hi Mr. Scott."
"Hi, Mel. How is the project going?"
"Well, I made contact with a friend of mine who was going to design school, to see about designing a logo, business cards, and stationary for the company."

I didn't get very far, when Mr. Scott interrupted.
"You know Mel; I really don't think that making car mats was a good idea for your thesis."

As he was talking and continued his reasoning, I didn't say a word. I unwrapped the package I brought into his office took out the mats and laid them on his desk. The mats were black, with his first initial and last name on it in yellow (matching the color of his car). In mid-stream of Mr. Scott's discourse of why aligning myself to a car mat manufacturer was a bad idea, he said,

"You know professors are not allowed to receive gifts from students."

I responded, "I am not giving you anything. I wanted to show you an example of the product, and besides, Mel the owner, said to give this to you."

"Are you sure the owner wanted me to have this?"
"Yes, he wanted to show his appreciation for letting me work with him. And besides, they aren't any good for anyone else. He would just have to throw them away."

"In that case, then it would be permissible for me to receive this. Please thank the owner for me. These are very attractive. Now I can understand why you wanted to work with Mel and his car mats. You have my full support."

With that I walked out with my approval for my thesis.

When I met Mel, he had been selling car mats off and on for three – four years and never got out of his garage; where he was using a pizza oven to melt the rubber for the mats. I worked with Mel for two years acting as a consultant to help him and to encourage him to expand his business. By the time I completed my thesis, the business was making enough money to support his brother, Robert, full time, they moved into a 3500-square foot store front and were now operating a continuous feed oven to speed production to meet increased demand.

I got an "A" on my thesis.

Stuntmen's Association Dinner Dance

My brother Wayne is a Stuntman and has been one for years. Perhaps the two most notable "doubles" that he performed for was Sidney Poitier and Clarence William III (photo) of the original Mod Squad. He has been in numerous movies; many I didn't even know about. When I was in high school, I would be with friends at the movies.

"Say, isn't that your brother? They would say.

"Yeah, it sure is." I would respond.

"Why didn't you tell us he was in the movie?"

"Didn't know"

Would be the typical lines. I often didn't know what movies my brother would be in. The Hollywood scene just did not interest me. However, I did go to one of the Stuntmen's Association Dinner Dance of which Wayne extended an invitation. It was at the Beverly Hilton in Beverly Hills. Renee, Ted, his date and another couple were with us. It was a very nice dinner, elegant and well attended.

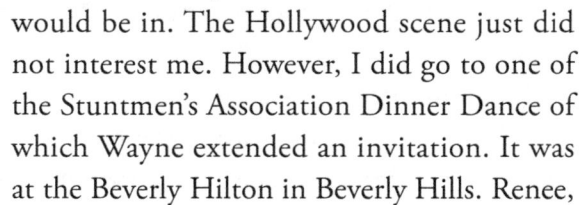

Sometime during the dinner, we were commenting about the Grammy's and the fact that it was having a dinner tonight at this same hotel. It wasn't long before someone suggested.

"Let's go see if we can find it; and, maybe, crash the party, huh?"

"You are looking for excitement, aren't you?" Someone else said.

"Well why not? This is nice, but maybe they'll have a few singers there we can meet."

"OK, I'm game. Let me let my brother know, in case he has to come bail us out of something," I said.

The six of us left our table and found our way into the catacombs that most hotels have. My experience in my youth came in handy here. I used to go into these kinds of passageways on a routine basis, especially at the museums. We entered the back hallways. Uncharacteristic to the manner in which I would have traversed the hallways, the group kept up a continuous chatter. Not surprising the talking got attention.

"What are you guys doing back here?" A hotel official said.

"Well, I think we are lost, and we are not sure where to go," I said.

"Well, where did you come from?" The official said.

"From that away." Ted and I both said.

Difference was, he pointed in the direction of the Stuntmen's Dinner, I pointed in the direction of what I hoped was the Grammy's Dinner. Fortunately, the official was looking at me and not at Ted.

"You guys can't be out roaming the halls like this. You gotta go back inside. Follow me."

The official turned around and started leading us to the Grammy's Dinner. Evidently, he didn't see Ted and where he was pointing. We got to one of the side doors to the dinner and he escorted us inside.

"If I see you guys in those hallways again, I will have to ask you to leave." The official said.

"Oh, we won't leave until the party's over," I said.

Now that we had crashed the party, all we had to do was find a table. We located a table that was one removed from Stevie Wonder and his entourage. We sat down and began to laugh at what we just pulled off. We looked around the room and saw a number of singers, I knew the faces, but not the names. We sat at the table for a short time, talking about the singers around us.

"Are you guys ready to scout out what's for dinner, or at least what's good for dessert?" I said.

"Yeah, I don't mind getting something." Ted said.

"OK, you guys go. Renee and I will mind the fort," I said.

The four of them went to check out the lay of the land. Upon their return, plates fully loaded, they had this look of amazement.

"Man, you wouldn't believe what they got. They got four carving stations, serving Prime Rib, Lobster Tails at your choosing, shrimp, pasta, Stuffed Crab and man, you gotta go see for yourself," Ted said.

Renee and I didn't waste any time. True enough, it was just as Ted described. Renee and I got our plates and went to go sit back down. On the way back to the table, we passed an alcove that had about 20 people in it. What we saw was fairly disgusting. Food was everywhere. It looked like they had a food fight. It was apparent that there was neither very little appreciation of the food that comprised the dinner, nor the invitation to attend. Couldn't help but think of spoiled little brats. However, we didn't let that spoil the dinner for us. We got back to the table and enjoyed the rest of the evening.

Renee's Run (Mountain High)

As you may have guessed by now that skiing is my favorite sport. Second to skiing is Wind Surfing; however, we'll save that story for another time. This is the story about "Renee's Run." We were skiing Mountain High, a ski resort in Wrightwood, CA, about 90 minutes east of Los Angeles. It was great ski conditions, a gorgeous day, sunny, and little to no wind. There was Vic, my sister, Renee, her sister Myrna, and a few others on the mountain just having a great time. Because of the conditions, everyone was skiing extremely well and became somewhat embolden. Earlier that morning, all of us would come down the mountain together until we came to a point where the trail would split into an intermediate and a double black diamond run. I would ski the double black diamond (See insert) or advance run while the others would ski the intermediate run.

On this one trip down the mountain, as I mentioned, everyone became emboldened and wanted to ski the run that I was taking. Mind you, the name of this run is called "The Olympian" and it is called that for a reason. It also is in full view of the lodge; and watching skiers come down this run is a favorite past time for those sitting in the lodge taking a break. The run is very steep and has a lot of bumps. We all ski to the top of the run and I say to them,

"It's OK to turn back, cause once you start, the only way from here is down."

"Well Mel, won't you start and show us how to do it."

"OK, I'll ski a quarter of the way down and all of you ski to that point."

I ski a little slower and make wider turns than I normally do so they can see how to navigate the bumps. Renee decides she is going to go first. Now Renee is wearing this bright red ski outfit with a red hat trimmed in white fur. She is looking really good in this bright red, so I know she could be seen by a lot of people in the lodge. She starts out clean, makes her first turn, looking good. She starts her second turn, catches the tip of her ski on one of the bumps and it spins her around. I am down the hill looking up at Renee as she spins out of sight, hidden by one of the bumps. (See insert, dash line.) The next time I see her she is on her back, coming head first down the mountain. Then she disappears again. The next thing I see is a ski go flying up in the air. Renee reappears, this time coming over the top of the bump sideways and then she disappears again. As she disappears, another ski does a pirouette skyward. As she reappears, this time on her stomach again, but coming down feet first, hands outstretched in the surrender position. She disappears again, this time goggles and hat appear and follow the skyward trajectory as the skis. Of course, I'm feeling helpless, since there was nothing I can do, being that I am down the mountain and not above her.

The next time she appears it is apparent that she is beginning to lose momentum, but no other gear or clothing, since whatever she could lose, was lost. Renee finally came to a halt about 20 yards above from where I am standing. I begin the arduous task of side stepping back up the mountain to make sure Renee is OK. A couple of expert skiers coming down the mountain evidently saw what happen and began picking up skis, poles (oh, yeah, she lost her poles on one the disappearances), goggles and hat. Renee lay motionless in the snow. I didn't know if she had broken something, if she was unconscious or what. I got there just as the guys collecting her things did. I didn't touch her, but asked,

"Do you hurt anywhere?" I asked.

"mmph, mmph."

"What? I can't hear you." I said.

"I said, just my pride. Let me lie here to get myself together." Renee replied.

Renee physically survived the run but paid a social price. With her red outfit and the spectacular fall and ride down the mountain, many a people in the lodge witnessed the event. Hence the name of the run is now unofficially called "Renee's Run." Oh, the others, once they found out Renee was OK, they sidestepped up the mountain, for a little way, and took the intermediate run.

Lake Tahoe

For seven straight years Renee and I would pull a group of 10 together, some would be repeaters, to make the 12-hour drive to Lake Tahoe in northern California. Through my job, I made contact with a couple that had a three-bedroom condo in South Lake Tahoe, about a 10-minute drive from Heavenly Valley Ski Resort and the casinos. We would leave Friday night after our volleyball game at Inglewood Park. Arrive in Tahoe Saturday morning, do grocery shopping and just have a leisurely day. During the week, the guys would get up before the gals and fix breakfast. We always planned to be at the ski resort by 7:30 AM, so the mornings would come early.

On one particular weekday, after a couple of days skiing, none of the gals wanted to get up. Time and time again we made the attempt. No movement. As a last resort, I got my tape player, cued up the "Rocky" theme and pushed the play button. It was ama-a-a-zing. My sister, Vic, raised straight up out bed. She didn't push herself up she just raised up, wow. That got the day started. Over the years, we had a great time, and we always had snow. Friday was the culmination of the trip. We would get up and ski as usual, but we would break around 3:00 PM to go to Harrah's casino and their seafood buffet. There would always be about a two hour wait, so all 10 of us would go get in line. After about 15 minutes, with all the laughter and noise we made, we knew people in line knew we were there. After 15 – 20 minutes, half of us would leave, go to the condo, shower, change clothes, and come back and get in line. Another 10 - 15 minutes of interaction, then the remaining half would repeat the process. By the time the second half returned, it was only a matter of minutes before we were seated for dinner. After dinner, we either saw a performance at one of the casinos or went to the movie theater. It didn't stop there. After the movie or performance, we would go bowling until about 2:00 AM. We all would be dragging back to the condo, but all saying how great a time we had. We would sleep in on Saturday, clean the condo, and leave around noon or 1:00 PM. It was always a great week.

A Trip to Washington (Back at Work)

There were 11 of us on my first trip to NAV-Air, in Washington DC. This was going to be my first big assignment as head of the negotiating team. The other 10 members were all white males with one exception, a black program manager that headed up the gyrotron program. These guys were veterans, had been to Nav-Air several times and had developed long time associations. Me, I was the new kid on the block, didn't know any of the Government guys and it would be my first trip to DC. It was exciting. We stayed at a Hyatt in Crystal City, a section of Washington, just south of the city. By this time, I became fairly close friends with one of the Program Managers, John, who was a runner. He was a big guy but liked to run. That first day of our arrival, we made plans to get up early and do a two to three-mile run. I wasn't necessarily a runner, but I ran a few miles a week and was in excellent physical shape. Three miles for any given run would be about my max.

We started out about 6:00 AM, which was 3:00 AM California time. We ran along the major artery packed with cars going into DC, across the Potomac Bridge and from there, toward the Mall. As we got to the Mall, John says "I've always wanted to circle the Washington Monument, let's do that then we'll head back." I thought, by the time we get to the monument, it will be over three miles.

And then there is the run back. But, I'm a trooper, so I agree. We circle the monument and head back to the hotel. It just so happens that on this side of the highway, there is the Pentagon.

"Oh, by gosh, there is the Pentagon. That is another icon I have always wanted to run around. Come on let's go, you're looking really good." John says.

"Yeah, right."

Somewhere in the back of my mind I'm thinking that I heard that the Pentagon was a mile in circumference. Just what I wanted, another mile. So off we go, heading toward the Pentagon. As we started around the Pentagon we passed a fairly large helicopter on the front lawn. At first, I thought maybe it was the President's helicopter, but it wasn't. It seemed like we ran and ran. As we turned the fourth corner, at least I thought I counted four, I was disappointed that I didn't see the helicopter. I turned to John.

I said, "I counted four corners, we should be seeing that helicopter."

John didn't say anything but just started laughing. I had no clue as to why he was laughing or what I had said that would make him laugh. By now my brain was not in gear, I was tired, and thirsty.

He looked at me and said, "Mel, we are running around the PENTAGON"

At that moment, it clicked. Five sides, not four.

"OK, I said something dumb. You better not repeat it," I said.

"I won't tell anyone," John said.

After about 8 - 10 miles, we finally made it back to the hotel (see prior photo for the whole route). As we were running up the steps to the hotel, the other guys were going to breakfast. We told them we would hurry and shower and join them. Wouldn't you know it, at breakfast, John told the guys about the four-sided pentagon. Of course, he set it up with the run, my tail dragging, tongue hanging out, eyes crossed, then I make this dumb comment. From that moment on, and for the rest of the trip, if anyone made a dumb comment, all they had to say was, "At least it wasn't a pentagon," and all attention would be diverted from them to me. Reminded me of a time in a far away country…when I made a comment about roosters.

That morning we walked into the Nav-Air office. The team hadn't been there for about 15 months, so it was like an old homecoming gathering. Everyone was shaking hands, making quick private comments, and in general, just catching up on old times. Everyone was engaged with someone. Everyone, except me. My team got so wrapped up in the excitement that they forgot to introduce me. Me, I was the youngest member of the team, so it would have been easy for the Nav-Air folks to assume I was an analyst or someone to assist in the negotiations. There was never any prior mention of me joining the team, so Nav-Air didn't know that I was even coming. After about 15 minutes, we, or I should say they (I was essentially shoved to the back of the crowd) began to fill the negotiating conference room. The room had a very long, rectangular table, seating for about 15 on a side.

My team walked in and took up position on the far side, facing the door. All the Nav-Air folks sat closest to the door. As I finally approached the door, my team had already positioned themselves as to where they were going to sit, except the center seat was left vacant. By this time, most of the Nav-Air team had their position and were beginning to sit. I walked into the room and immediately felt all eyes from the Nav-Air team focus on me. They saw the Hughes team sitting, center seat vacant. The importance of the center seat is, that is the person who will lead the negotiations. That is the person that will do most of the talking, will lead any rebuttals, will make any offers and will ultimately close the deal. The room got instantly quiet on the Nav-Air side. My guys continued their subdued discussions, oblivious to the drama that was being played out. The reason for the Nav-Air reaction was that they had no clue as to who I was, the authority of the role I would play, my temperament, likes or dislikes, yet they were going to have to deal with me. My team had already filled me in on the Nav-Air team, so I was ready for them. They were not ready for me.

As I walked around the table, it was if every Nav-Air head was being controlled by the same string, they swiveled in unison. I turned the back corner and began walking past each one of my guys until I got to the center chair, and, I'm sure to their horror, I pulled back the chair. There was still silence on the Nav-Air team for several seconds, when a very sharp analyst spoke up, addressed his lead.

He said, "Jack, I forgot some very important notes, can we wait five minutes before we get started so that I may get them?"

Jack, the Nav-Air lead jumped on the request really quick. This would be an opportunity to take time out to find out who I was.

"Sure Bill, we can give you about 15 minutes. We'll take a short break until you return."

Jack acknowledged the request to delay and stood up from his chair. He motioned to one of my guys, someone with whom he was well acquainted, and asked him to join him outside the room. Shortly thereafter, I was asked to join them. We had a very successful negotiation.

The next year, only six of us went back to negotiate. The following year, and subsequent years thereafter, only I and the two program managers and a contracts guy went back to Nav-Air to negotiate. A total of four of us, down from 11 my first year. Once again, my financial, industrial engineering and manufacturing experience paid off. I could talk finance and tie it together with the manufacturing process to present a very reasonable argument for our position. We did very well at the negotiations.

As I said we did very well at the negotiations. I saved the company money by reducing the number of people flying back to Washington, reduced the manpower required for preparation, and reduced the percentage lost during negotiations. Once again, I had proven that I was capable of operating outside my job classification and demonstrated that "Black can make a difference." However, once again, was there any special recognition? Was there any monetary compensation? Nada. I'm in Finance and what I was doing was primarily a Contracts job. "Civilians don't often appreciate nor reward leadership, innovation, or dedication. The service does and has recognized innate leadership in you; which, will not necessarily be so in the civilian sector where politics and envy can come into play." (General Olds, Commandant, U. S. Air Force Academy)

The First Desktop PC

As I was preparing a proposal for a contract, I thought, there has to be a better, more efficient way to do this. It was 1979, and the only electronic options that were available was a Xerox word processing station and a couple of entry level computers such as the Commodore 64 and a very unsophisticated Apple II. I wanted a computer, but the cost required that I get some of the other financial departments involved to share the expense. I polled the other Finance Managers and asked what they would prefer, a computer or the word processing station. To a person they all said the word processing station.

Uncommon II: Black Can Make a Difference

I called Xerox and asked them to do a demo. The guy came in, set up the unit. Very impressive. He then asked each manager how they believed they would be able to use the unit. Each manager said that they didn't think they could use it and saw no value in it for them. I was extremely disappointed. Had they been honest with me at first, I would not have had this demo set up. I apologized to the Xerox representative for having him come out unnecessarily. Afterwards, I went to the controller and told Dick that regardless of the other managers, I needed something to automate what we were doing. He gave me the green light to explore. It wasn't long before I came across the Commodore 64.

The C64 took its name from its 64 Kilobytes (65,536 bytes) of RAM and had favorable sound and graphical specifications when compared to contemporary systems such as the Apple II at a price that was well below the circa US $1200 demanded by Apple. I spent two months investigating and working out a deal to make a purchase. I was within one day of closing the deal on the C64 when IBM made the announcement that they were introducing the desktop PC. I had to make a choice. Do I continue with the Commodore 64, or do I go with IBM? I chose to go with IBM. It would mean a two-month delay, but I figured IBM was going to be around for a while, so I placed my bet with the big guy. I went to an electronics store called, "Comupustop" to order and pick up the computer. The system was so new that a printer was not ready for it. The guys at the computer store were really sharp and were able to get a printer called Paper Tiger to work with the new PC.

The system cost over $4000, had a single sided, 256K, 7.25-inch floppy disc drive, with a processing speed of about 256K. It was the very first desktop IBM PC purchased at Hughes. I sat the unit in a common area for our team. Initially, I was the one using it the most. It didn't take long however, until I had to have a sign-up sheet to limit time and access. The unit was getting such heavy usage that ultimately, the sign-up sheet had to be modified to include after hours and weekends. It didn't take long either for the Controller to put the PC on his "must see" list, for whenever he had visitors. He wanted to show them "his" computer. He also would pull out the sign-up sheet and brag about the after hours and weekend usage. There were many heated discussions over the use of this one computer that no one initially wanted but me. The other managers finally began to see its value and put in a request for a unit of their own.

Meeting with Division President

After a few years in my position as Head of Pricing & Estimating, things were running fairly smoothly and I wanted another challenge. I approached Dick and requested to have an opportunity to speak to the Division President. Not that I wanted to leave the division, I just wanted to open doors for people to gain senior level positions, other than engineers. I had been with the division about two years now and had briefly met the president one time before. I doubted that he would remember me. I entered his suite, five minutes ahead of the appointed time, and his admin, Nancy, warmly greeted me. Her, I knew very well and would often exchange pleasantries when we met in the hall or cafeteria. She called the President, Nick, to let him know that I had arrived. By her reaction on the phone, it was obvious that he had questioned her on why I was so early. She did a good job of recovery, but it was clear that he was not looking forward to this discussion.

I wasn't sure how much information Dick, my boss, had conveyed about why I wanted to meet with him. One thing for certain, if Dick did not let him know, one of the things that would be on his mind is, "Why would a Black manager want to see me unless there is some racial problem." At the appointed time, I knocked on his door. He greeted me and offered me the chair facing his desk. He went back around his desk to sit down.

"Mind telling me the purpose of this meeting. Dick didn't say."

I told him, "I would like to know what can be done to open up opportunities to gain higher positions to those managers that don't have engineering degrees. Since I am one of the few managers that have an MBA, I felt that I was in the best position to ask the question."

With that comment, his face visibly relaxed. This was obviously a question he felt comfortable with.

He got up from his chair.

"Come, let's sit on the sofa and talk." The President said.

He was really relaxed. I followed him to the sofa and sat down.

"Rather than talk generalities, let's talk about you."

"I don't want to talk about me," I said.

I wanted to change policy, not an instance.

"But I want to talk about you," he said.

With that, I had to agree with him or essentially the meeting was over. We spent about 40 minutes together, with him having a better appreciation of my contribution to the success of his division. Still, I didn't get what I came for. It was too much within the culture of Hughes to promote people with engineering degrees than those without. Whenever I saw Nick after that meeting, he would make a point to stop, say, "Hi" and ask a few questions of what I was working on.

An embarrassing moment.

One day I went to a retirement lunch with about thirty other people at a local restaurant. The seating was pretty much in a "U" shape, with some tables in the middle. I was sitting along one of the legs of the "U," in a booth. There were several ladies and one other guy in the booth with me. Both of us guys were at the end of the booth. Just as we finished lunch, the retiree got up to speak. Because of how I was sitting, I had to turn a little in my seat, with my back to the rest of the people in my booth. Before I continue the story, I have to divert and tell you about Renee and I when I take her to dinner. When we go to dinner, rarely do I sit across from Renee, but I will sit next to her. Oftentimes, when in a booth, at a dinner show, or when something else has my/ our attention, I will put my hand on Renee's leg. The contact is to let her know I'm still thinking of her in spite of the diversion. It is such a habit that I do it unconsciously.

By now I guess you know what's coming. Yep. While I was focused on the comments of the retiree, I shifted my position and unconsciously put my hand on the leg of the lady sitting next to me. I still had my back to her and the others in the booth so I didn't give it any thought. Now you would think the lady would have said something, but she didn't. I don't know how long I was in this position, but it was more than five minutes. Now you can imagine how I felt when I discovered what I was doing. Fortunately, the way the seating was, no one else could see where my hand was, only the lady I was sitting next to.

"Oh boy. Gee, I am so sorry. You see when I go out with my wife, I have this habit of placing my hand on her leg, and ..."

"Mel, don't worry about it. I didn't take offense," she said.

I was in such a predicament. I didn't want to make a big fuss about it, because others would hear and begin asking questions. Yet, I wanted the lady to know that I was sincerely apologetic. In the end, she just looked at me.

"Remember, you owe me one."

I didn't want to ask, "One what?"

Finance Manager

Since the meeting with Nick didn't effect a change, I asked Dick again about other opportunities.

"Hmmm, well, there is this R&D department that I have not been able to get under control, cost wise. I have sent manager, after manager in that department to help them with their cost but all were unsuccessful. Do you think you want to take a shot at it?" Dick said.

I did. After about two months with the department and unbeknownst to me, the Department VP came to Dick and asked if I could be transferred to their department. They liked what I was doing so well that they wanted me to become part of their organization. Dick told them that I had another assignment in two months but that I could spend that time training my replacement. After this assignment was up Dick wanted me to work with another department and essentially do the same thing that I did with the R&D department. I did. After about three months, the department VP came to Dick and he also asked if I could be transferred to his organization. I was succeeding where many before me had failed. Dick wouldn't release me, but in this instance, had me on indefinite loan to their organization. Eventually, I got promoted to a Finance Manager position.

As Government Liaison, I had responsibility to respond to any Government audit questions that was submitted to the division. When I became a Finance Manager, this was one of the functions dropped from my responsibility; until we did poorly in an audit. As the division was trying to recover from that audit, I was asked to re-engage. These audits are very serious since the failure of an audit can bar the company from bidding on any Government contracts. And when the only business a company has is Government business, passing these audits become critical. I took the lead once again and was successful in resolving all the Government issues. As a result, this function, Government Liaison, was re-attached as part of my job description. You would think that I would have received something for this effort, but you know the trend – nada.

Tour Guide

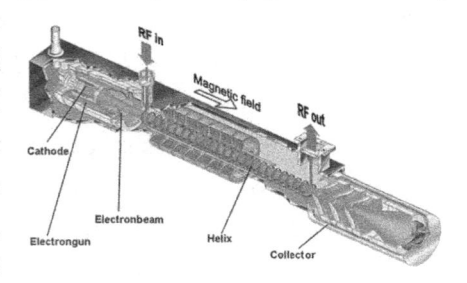

As a Finance Manager, I dropped many of my prior ancillary functions such as Government Liaison (temporarily) and Lead Negotiator (also temporary), but I continued as the Company's Tour Guide. The tour guide function came about totally unplanned. One day we had about 7 - 8 Government folks in to tour the facility. I was part of the welcoming committee. As we took the group on tour, they began to ask questions of the engineer. The answers that he gave resulted in them having the "deer in the headlight look." I began to breakdown the engineers comment into layman's language. It didn't take very long that they began to ask me questions rather than the engineer. When we returned back to the meeting room, several of the Government people told my management about how I was able to simplify the manufacturing process and that they were very appreciative that I was part of the group. From that day, until I left the company, I became the tour guide of choice. Even today I could give you the rudiments on the working of a Traveling Wave Tube or TWT as they are called. However, a discussion on electrons, attenuations, pulse gain, permanent magnets shadow grid, cathodes, and anodes wouldn't be very exciting, unless you were in the field.

As mentioned, Lead negotiator for the division was also put aside as one of my functions, when I became a Finance Manager, until the division was negotiating with one of our sister divisions, one in which I had worked previously. Mel was the program manager, in the other division, for the F-15 Radar program. Our division built the TWT and several other components for the radar. The two divisions were in heavy negotiations with each other and getting nowhere. I was in a meeting with the people who were negotiating, on another subject, when I heard about the stalemate. I asked if they needed assistance. The people in the room, a VP, a couple of directors, and managers looked around at each other, as if to say, "Why didn't we think to do this before?" After the initial silence, there was an outburst of conversation.

"Whoa, whoa, let me ask some questions first. The first one is, where are we in the negotiations and how far apart are we?"

Mel had a reputation in our division as a stubborn, long-time curmudgeon and was difficult to negotiate with. I informed the group that I knew Mel quite well and that I would be willing to take on the challenge. They all agreed to let me take the lead. After the meeting, on my own, I called Mel.

"Hey Mel, how are things? You really got a reputation here; did you know that?"

He laughed at their perception of him as I told him their description of him.

"I know that you really are a pussy cat, but I won't tell them that. What they don't know is that they just have to have the right kind of catnip."

"Ha, Ha, Ha. Very funny but true. So why the call? Are they getting you involved?"

"Yes, they are."

I told Mel what was happening on this end and that I was going in as lead. I told him where we needed to be and asked if he could get there. This number was more than the number at which they were at a stalemate.

He hesitated a little and then said "For you Mel, and for my namesake, yes."

We then began to strategize on how the call would proceed. Of course, he had to stay in character and not get to the bottom line too quickly; we wouldn't want to ruin his image. The next day I placed a conference call to Mel with the VP and two other managers in the room. Mel was being true to form, he didn't have to try very hard, so much so that I began to wonder if he remembered our conversation from yesterday. We bickered back and forth going nowhere.

Finally, I said, "You curmudgeon old goat, you can take your contract and shove it. See if your darn radar will work without our unit. They'll strap you in the plane instead. Give us a call when you are ready to do business."

At that Mel began to laugh. It was good that he did, because the faces on this end were in total shock and disbelief. I was so out of character; and, this was a customer.

After Mel stopped laughing, he said, "Now we're getting somewhere. All I wanted was honesty."

After this exchange, it didn't take long to come to an agreement. We reached an agreed amount that our team thought would never happen. Mel was pleased with the numbers and our side was more than happy. Later that day, Mel called me.

"Hey Buddy, how did I do?"

"You know; you are a curmudgeon old goat. You had me wondering if you even remembered our conversation yesterday. I didn't know if you had gone senile on me or not. Boy were you good."

"Good, I like making people work. You worked hard and I thank you for making it happen. Stop in to see me next time you're over this way."

Mel and I met several times to negotiate other contracts and the respect we had for one another only increased. As a result of my effort with negotiating with Mel, the division once again asked if I would take the banner as lead negotiator. Reward for this effort – nada.

Remember I am only one of three Black mangers in the whole division. Have demonstrated multiple of times that I can and have contributed significantly to the bottom-line of the division. I would have liked to have been recognized as an individual, but rarely is that the case if you are Black. The establishment has this propensity of categorizing "people of color" as one group. With that awareness, of categorizing, I always wanted to demonstrate that "Black can make a difference."

Thoughts

This pattern would repeat throughout my career; Due to my "uncommon" approach to solving issues, organizations would not fully appreciate my talent until it was no longer available to them. I believe this is in part due to my temperament. Because I try not to stress out over a situation and try to look at an issue objectively, it may seem to an observer that the problem was no big deal; whereas, in reality, the issue may have been huge, however, I do give thanks to God for wisdom. The audit and negotiation situation were two of many examples in my career, where someone or an organization took what I did for granted only to discover that it was not as easy as I may have made it look. It could be said that Mel and I collaborated on the F-15 deal, and that would be correct. However, it was the many years working with Mel and his being able to trust me that enabled that negotiation to be successful. Moreover, subsequent negotiations did not have a preceding phone call. I also think that some people either thrive or purposely create fire drills, just so they can gain attention in putting them out. Me, with proper planning, I rather avoid them.

The "Crew"

Eventually, Renee and I had joined Crenshaw Christian Center and became active members. I joined the camera crew; she became involved with the Women's Fellowship and Intercessory Prayer group. Occasionally on the "Crew" as we called ourselves, we would play a prank on Pastor Fred. We had four cameras in operation, but sometimes we would lose power to a camera. These were the cathode ray tube models, prior to solid state technology. When this happens, we would hold up a sign that would say, "Camera 2 is down." Pastor Fred knew which camera was camera 2 and would shy away from that position. One Sunday morning, just before we began recording the service for television, we held up a sign that said, "Camera 3 is down." No problem, this was not out of the ordinary. Shortly thereafter, we held up a sign that said, 'Camera 4 is down." OK, a little unusual, but we have had two cameras go down before. "Camera 1 is down." At this point, with a huge smile on his face, Pastor walks over to the closest camera and sticks his tongue out. With that we all lost it. There was so much laughter in the control room it took us a while to regain composure to start the program.

Pastor Fred didn't let it go at just sticking his tongue out, he got even with us in a very subtle way. This facility had columns to support the main roof and additional seating of about 100 people. It was within the building but outside of the main structure. Pastor Fred would often go to the left side of the auditorium, face the addition and address the people in this area. Problem was, getting to this position, Pastor Fred would have to pass a supporting column. In order to show a smooth transition, without him being blocked out by a column, it took three cameras to do so. Timing was critical. During the sermon, Pastor Fred made his way to his favorite spot when addressing the "addition" folks. He stood talking for a few moments then gathered himself as he usually does (to let us know he is about to walk) and took a step. . . My finger was on the switch button ready to transfer cameras . . . and he returned back to his position. We saw a slight smile creep across his face. He gathered himself again, I am ready again. He took a step. This time I was going to use the fader bar, it makes for a smoother transition and can give extra time to cover his move. He returned again to his original position. At this point we knew it was "get even time." On his third move, he completed the steps and we were out of trouble. He confessed to the congregation what he did and continued to chuckle about it.

On any given Sunday, Pastor Fred could expect the unexpected. We had moved to our temporary sanctuary, the auditorium, on the new campus. Pastor Fred was on stage giving some announcements when Gary looked at me and said, "Mel you got the helm." Whenever the Director is preoccupied, the Technical Director (TD) always takes over.

"Time to execute our 'Remove and Replace' project. Gary said.

Gary made his way down the back way to the stage and came out from behind the curtain, to Pastor Fred's right and slightly behind him. Pastor noticed that he lost the attention of the people and turned to see what everyone was looking at. Now it is very unusual for the Director to come on stage and Pastor Fred knew this. At the sight of Gary, Pastor obviously asked if anything was wrong.

"Gary, are we OK for taping? Is something wrong?"

"No nothing is wrong. But everything will be even better in just a second." Gary said.

What Pastor didn't know was that David, a six foot five, 270 lb. member of the Crew, and Rosie Greer were approaching him. They came upon Pastor Fred from behind, picked him up by his elbows and carried him off the stage, feet dangly. As they passed by Gary, Pastor in tow, Gary smiled and waved. The congregation went wild. Gary proceeded to go to the podium and began to do the announcements in a Pastor Fred imitation. At this the congregation stood and cheered. Pastor Fred watched from the side of the stage where Dave and Rosie had dropped him off. Pastor Fred eventually took back control; not without threatening to banish Gary to 40 years in the desert.

Pastor Fred enjoyed these little interchanges with the crew. We knew he did because never once did he ever rebuke us or tell us to quit.

Renee and I had been married for four years and now we were expecting our first child. On this particular Sunday, I was at church, Renee wasn't feeling too well, and was at home. We had just started recording the Sunday service when we got a call into the control room that Renee needed to go to the hospital. Prince was directing and I was the Technical Director (TD) at the time. I preferred the TD position because that was where the action took place. Nothing went on air unless the TD made it happen. The TD has to press the right buttons and move the switches to have the right image displayed. The Director calls the shots, which camera will go live and which will not, and has overall responsibility for the program. The Director and TD often sit side by side.

When we got the call, Prince got so excited that he forgot that we were taping. I began directing while performing my TD functions.

"OK, let's go to camera 2 for the wide shot. Camera 2 we are going to be on you for a while so do a slow zoom in but hold it steady. Cable puller on 2, standby to relieve Gary on camera 3. Gary, when your replacement comes, I need you to come back and relieve me at TD."

About then Pastor begins to walk over to a part of the church where a pillar exists and we can lose him from camera 2.

"OK, guys, Pastor is not cooperating. Of course, he doesn't know what's happening so we have to work with it. Hold on 3, Gary we are going to have to come to you until Pastor leaves the area. OK, 3 make the change, quick. Two, you're hot, keep it steady and continue the slow zoom."

When Gary showed up, Prince was just starting to regain his composure. I immediately left to get Renee to the hospital. Aaron was born about 11:00 PM that same day. It was Father's Day, 21 June 1982.

I was the Technical Director for seven years with the Crew and never missed a Sunday except for one day a year, when we went skiing at Lake Tahoe. I say this only to emphasize the dedication many of the crew members had. There were a lot of Sundays that we would be at church, by 4:30 AM, pulling out cameras, cables, TV monitors and such. We were really pioneers in the Televangelist arena. Most pastors preached from behind a pulpit. Not Pastor Fred, he moved. Many times, visitors would come to the church and see pillars. They would comment that they didn't see pillars on television and didn't know the church had pillars. We were always glad to hear this as that result is what we strive for every Sunday. Because of his moving, Pastor Fred didn't make it easy for us. We were neophytes performing at a level beyond our experience and didn't know it. The only way we found out about our performance was the result of a couple of visitors. The Moody Institute sent a couple of people out to observe how we were producing the show; and, they expressed their amazement that we didn't have but one professional on the crew, his name was Walter. That one professional was crucial during taping though. He would color balance the cameras on the fly so that the audience wouldn't see Pastor looking like a ghost on one camera and have a Florida tan on another. It was a very critical position.

When I left to go to Orlando, I would come back every other weekend to see Renee and the children. On those weekends, I would perform my usual Technical Director function. On one Sunday, Walter, the one professional, wasn't able to show. Gary, Prince, Duke and I (the Crew leaders) got together to determine if we were going to tape the services for this Sunday.

"No need to cancel the taping. I can do the job," I said.

"Mel, you haven't been trained in that function."

"Not officially no. Remember when we couldn't get a signal to the overflow room and I took the whole console apart and re-wired it? I hadn't been officially trained for that either. But I got the job done. I can do this."

"Ok, let's prepare to roll tape. Let's get everybody on station."

We had a clean taping that Sunday, and I was glad that it was on a Sunday I was in town.

Japan – 1984

While working for the Western Regional VP of Trans World Airlines,

Renee was rewarded for her effort and contribution to a March of Dimes campaign. The reward was an airline flight to Japan and three days in the Akasaka Prince Hotel (AP) in Tokyo, Japan. The flight to Japan was 14 hours, so I spent some of the time reading the pamphlet, "Learning how to Speak Japanese." This proved to be, both, to our embarrassment and benefit while in Japan. The AP hotel had recently been built and was only six months old. It was about 35 stories tall and we had a room on the 33rd floor. The view was phenomenal. The lobby of the hotel was all marble and had a huge carving of a Jade Chinese Junk, about eight feet long, and a very ornate chandelier suspended over a marble staircase. From the main floor of the lobby, and going down to the Ice Cream Parlor, there was a marble Grand Piano on one of the landings. It was the most impressive lobby we had ever seen. We felt and acted like the "Rich and Famous."

We walked into our room and was instantly impressed with the décor, the view, and accouterments. There were, toothpaste, toothbrushes, deodorant, cologne, perfume, lotion and even His and Hers slippers and bathrobes. Nice. Next to the bed there was a row of light switches. Two switches controlled the lights in the room, one controlled the sheer curtain, another switch controlled the blackout curtain, and one I couldn't tell at all what it did; and, this was in 1984.

As we ventured out, we went looking for a "Banzai" tree. We went to a couple of department stores and were impressed with the elevator girls. Young school age girls, wearing white gloves. You tell them which floor and they push the buttons for you. At one department store I figured I would try out my newly learned Japanese. We went up to a store clerk and I asked, in Japanese.

"Do you have Banzai trees?"

The clerk immediately began to giggle. She couldn't contain herself, so much so that she attracted the attention of another clerk. When the other clerk came over to inquire, the giggling clerk told her why she was giggling. The second clerk called a third clerk over. Renee and I looked on in amusement. When they finally got their composure, they began to apologize, as it is not their custom to insult someone by laughing at them. I told them we were not offended and was amused at their behavior. Anyhow, they offered us a gift as an appeasement. The gift was valued around $20 in then dollars, so I didn't mind them laughing at all. The department store did not have any Banzai trees.

Renee and I were having lunch with a tour group at a Martial Arts School, watching about 75 students go through their drills. I hadn't given up trying to speak Japanese so I thought I would make another attempt. As the waitress came to our table I said,

"Me su wo kudasai? Arrigato guzai masta." (May I have some water please? Thank you very much.)

At least that's what I thought I said. Our tour guide immediately jumped up from his table and said, "Who said that?"

It got really quiet. Mind you, we are at a martial arts school, 75 students and about 10 instructors were present. In my ignorance, did I offer a challenge? What did I say this time? Did I offend? This was not the place to offend anybody.

Do I confess it was me?" Fortunately, another American tourist asked,

"What was it that was said?"

"Someone asked for a glass of water." The tour guide said.

Knowing that, I sheepishly raised my hand.

"Where did you learn to speak Japanese? That was excellent. I have not heard it spoken that well, by an American, in a long time."

With relief, I said, "I learned it on the flight on the way here to Japan"

"On the plane on the way here to Japan? Incredible. That is hard to believe. You did well."

Ahh, redemption is such a good feeling.

On another outing, Renee and I met with the TWA Regional Manager (Frank), who is Japanese and his wife for dinner. They came by the hotel to pick us up and we drove to downtown Tokyo. Space in Tokyo is at a premium, both land and roads. The streets all have bumper to bumper traffic, but no bent bumpers. It is against the law to drive a damaged vehicle on the road. As we arrived at our destination and got out of the car, a valet was there to assist the ladies. Frank started to escort us to a nearby restaurant when I asked for him to wait for just a minute. I wanted to see what was going to happen with the car. I saw no parking garage. We had pulled into, what looked like to me a little alley, so I saw no place to park a car. As I stood there watching, the valet got into the car, pulled forward into what looked like a little cage. He got out of the car, came back to his station and pulled a lever. Amazing, Amazing. The car and cage began to move sideways and slightly upward. It was as if the car was on a giant ferris wheel, squished in the middle. There is minimal room horizontally, so the Japanese have gone vertically. As the car moved, it made room for the next car. I left shaking my head in amazement.

The Japanese, although quite modern, still keep many of the old traditions. As a foreigner, or commoner, you or I would go to a restaurant and have a seat in the common area. If you have a little prestige, you would be permitted to go through a door and sit at one of the tables in this second room. Now if you really have prestige or connections, there is the ultimate backroom. Since we were with Frank, we were escorted through two doors to have a seat in the most prestigious spot in the restaurant. It was obvious that this restaurant catered not only to the elite Japanese, but also catered to high-class Americans or Europeans. Sunken wells existed around some of the table, to put your legs in, to accommodate foreigners. We sat at one of these tables. The ambiance was superb. Subdued lighting throughout, but small recessed spotlights over the eating area. Renee and I especially liked the small stream that was in front of us and surrounded our table, very attractive.

Frank of course did the ordering, so Renee and I just relaxed and enjoyed the company of Frank, his wife, and the superb ambience. It wasn't too long when Frank said our appetizers are coming. I looked up to see what the waitress was carrying and didn't see a waitress. Frank began to chuckle at the very obvious puzzled look on my face.

"The waitress is not bringing our food, the water is. See the larger stream over there? Our food is on a little boat, floating on that stream. When it gets to our location, a small gate will open up and divert the boat down the little stream surrounding our table and bring the food to us." Frank said.

Sure 'nuff. It happened just like Frank said. Renee and I were beyond being impressed. The first thing that arrived were extremely thin slices of Kobe beef. They were arrayed as the tail of a peacock, while the body was formed out of, I don't know. All I know is that we ate it and it tasted extremely delicious. We took our chop sticks and picked up the meat and we swish-swished it in a hot cast iron pot that was sitting on top of a small coal fire (By the way, this arrived by boat as well). How we liked our meat was dependent on how long we swish-swished the meat in the water. The shorter we swished, the rarer the meat. A short time later, another boat came, this time with vegetables, also nicely arrayed. By now the water that we had been swishing in had a deep brown color and was flavored with all the swishing. Frank took the vegetables and put them in the pot. Beef vegetable soup. It was more than yummy. The whole experience, the meal, and evening was just fabulous.

Something Strange Happened

Prior to the birth of Aaron, Renee and I often times were invited to multiple events happening the same day or weekend. In fact, one friend, before he knew us, and when he first heard our name, he thought it was one person. When people spoke about us, it was always "Melandrenee," there was hardly a pause between the two names. Since we didn't have children, we were very spontaneous, helpful, and dependable. Our friends took note and didn't hesitate to invite us to help with an event or to just come over and socialize. However, once Aaron was born, these invites dropped about 30%. Then when Desiree was born, it dropped another 50%. Also, we noticed that we began to hang out with other moms and dads that had children about the same age as Aaron and Dez. It is strange how these innocent little creatures can affect your whole lifestyle.

Aaron

One thing that I have a very vivid memory of, while Renee was in labor during Aaron's birth, was a marathon back massage. Renee had what was called, "back labor." I guess it is called this when the baby presses against the spinal cord and causes pain and irritation. We discovered early on in her labor, while at the hospital, that massaging her back would give her some relief from this pain and irritation. After about 8 – 10 minutes of the massage, she was good for about 20 minutes. This went on for about 10 hours. I thought, "If I have to do this massage thing much longer, I'm going after the boy." Finally, when Aaron showed up, I was surprised how cute he looked. Even the nurses made comment about how unusual it is that a baby would look as cute as Aaron when first born. Although they attempted to get Aaron to cry, he wouldn't.

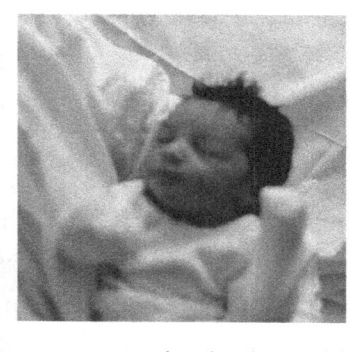

They finally gave up when they laid him on his stomach and he raised his head to look at them (rarely does a newborn have the strength to raise their head).

Aaron was about 14 months old and like most toddlers, very inquisitive. One morning, after a party in our home the night before, Aaron was up and about and appeared to be fascinated at all the decorations hanging around. Renee and I were coming out of our bedroom when we spotted him. We stopped and began peeking from the hallway. He was looking, touching, and having a great time exploring. His exploration brought him close to an object that obviously was more fascinating than everything else. It was a little higher than he was tall and it bobbled a little. As he got closer to it, it moved a little. At first it moved away from him, then it began to return to its original position. Aaron was obviously surprised at this movement and began to back away. As he backed away, the object began to move in his direction. Aaron continued to back away and the object continued to follow him. As Aaron's little legs began to move faster, so did this object. At one point, it came to Aaron's awareness that backing up was not going to be fast enough. He turned around … feet help the body… and began running. Next thing we heard was, "Maaaama."

Aaron was still a toddler and was just barely tall enough to reach the top of the kitchen counter. Because of dishes, knives or forks that may be on the counter, he was frequently told not to run his hand across the kitchen counter. However, boys will be boys. Early one morning, Renee was in the kitchen mixing frosting for a cake. She left the kitchen for a moment and Aaron, playing in the living room, saw his opportunity. After she was out of sight, wouldn't you know it, he ran into the kitchen and began to run his hand across the counter tops. For some reason Aaron was not aware that I was nearby and followed him, at least to the kitchen doorway. I motioned for Renee to join me. Since nothing dangerous was on the counter we let him continue. He had passed on one side of the kitchen and was now on the other side, coming toward us. His arm fully extended, hand just barely clearing the top and… Whop! His hand hit the stirring spoon Renee was using for the frosting and it wacked him across the face and mouth. He yelped in surprise and began hollering … until he accidently tasted the frosting. His face lit up with a big grin and began looking around for the spoon. Renee and I were laughing so hard we forgot to admonish him.

Desiree

I had just come home from work, kissed Renee, and started playing with Aaron.

It wasn't too long before Renee came into the living room saying, "My back hurts a little, I think I have to go to the bathroom."

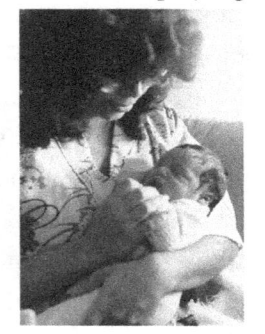

"Oh no you don't. Call your mom, let her know we're bringing Aaron over and I'm taking you to the hospital," I said.

"But I think I really have to go."

"Well, you are going to have to wait."

I grabbed the prepared overnight bag, put Renee in the car, got Aaron strapped in, and got the extra car seat that was given to us at a baby shower. We dropped Aaron off at Renee's mom and proceeded to rush (carefully) to the hospital. We no sooner got Renee in the hospital sat her in a wheel chair, that her water broke. The labor for Desiree was not nearly as long nor as painful as the time with Aaron. Even for me, I didn't have to do the marathon back massage.

It Still Happens

One of the guys, Dave, that was on the Crew, was a manager with

Xerox. One day he casually mentioned that Xerox had a position open for a senior level manager position. I told him I would be interested and brought in my resume to be submitted for consideration. After a couple of weeks went by with no contact, I asked Dave if he heard anything.

"Hey Dave, heard anything from the resume I gave you?"

"Come to think of it, no I had not. I 'll check this week for you." The next week, Dave told me about the conversation he had with the hiring Director. Dave said he approached the Director and asked the Director about the resume that he gave him.

The director responded, "Oh, that resume. I'm looking for someone with a degree."

"He does have a degree." Dave said

"But I need someone with supervisory experience."

"He has that; he is a manager of a department."

"But I really need someone with an advanced degree."

"He has an MBA from Loyola."

"Well, I think I already have someone in mind."

What the Director didn't say was, "I'm not interested in hiring someone that is Black."

Since Dave was Black, the Director assumed that any resume that Dave gave him would be from a Black individual. Also, the Director assumed that a Black individual would not have all the qualifications that he trumped up, such as a Bachelor's degree or supervisory experience, let alone having a Masters and already being a manager. The more things change, the more they stay the same.

"Mel, what's your take on the response from the Director?" Dave asked.

"You know Dave, I think a lot of times people, let's say Caucasians, are not intentionally prejudice, they just feel comfortable hiring people that look like them, talk like them, and act like them. Unfortunately, we have to deal with the fact that it is mostly Caucasians that are in the hiring and firing positions, which means, we have to be so much better than our Anglo peers. The "Glass Ceiling" exist, we, as a people, need to find those individuals who are willing to reach "down" through the glass to give us an opportunity. The hiring Director for instance, he wasn't brave enough to take the chance, even though he was presented with a qualified candidate; and I suspect, I have more experience than the person they settled on. The Director, like most managers will take the easy way out; and unfortunately, most managers are not good managers, so when you throw a different culture at them, they really lose it. I find that I spend a lot of my time un-training employees/ associates, in their expectation, of which they have acquired over the years, of managers, However, I have to always believe that it is their loss, not mine."

During my time with Hughes, at the second division, we gained a Black manager and lost one due to retirement. The count, including myself, remained at three. It wasn't just at Hughes. The whole time I was negotiating with Nav-Air, I never saw one Black person in a significant position of authority. Black individuals that I did see, and had a chance to speak with, were surprised that I was the lead negotiator. No other group, from any other company, that came in to Nav-Air even had a Black person on the team. Unfortunately, my being the only Black person during the negotiating process held true when we negotiated with our subcontractors as well.

A Call

Since we now had two children, Aaron and Desiree, Renee and I began to think about the challenges of raising children in LA. Los Angeles was changing and not in a way that we thought would be conducive to raising children. We talked about other cities and San Diego became a strong candidate. I was at work one day when I received a call from a head hunter.

"May I speak to Mel King," the Head Hunter said.

"This is Mel speaking," I said.

"Hi Mel, my name is Chuck, I'm an Executive Recruiter, and I am looking at your resume and I am very impressed with your experience."

And then he asked me the one question that totally surprised me.

He said, "How would you like to go for an interview in San Diego."

"San Diego, my wife and I were just talking about moving to San Diego. Of course, certainly I would like to interview in San Diego."

"Will you be able to go to San Diego this Friday?"

"Friday is not a good day for me. I have a couple of very important meetings that I am presiding over."

"I can go down on Saturday if that is possible."

"Well, I don't know. Let me call the person that is doing the interviewing and ask."

I hung up with the expectation that Chuck would call me back as soon as he knew if Saturday was OK. I figured it would take a day.

Chuck called me back within 15 minutes.

"Hi Mel, Saturday is OK, but you'll have to be there by 9:00 AM. He said he really liked your resume as well and said that he will be willing to meet with you if you can come early."

San Diego is two hours from LA. That meant I had to leave at 6:30 AM to assure that I find the hotel, parking, or allow for any road construction. That Saturday I met with the Interviewer. He was from Martin Marietta. I remember a Martin Marietta facility along the Harbor freeway in Torrance, just south of LA. I didn't know that they had a facility in San Diego. The interview went well, and I liked the interviewer.

When we completed the interview, he said, "I would like for you to fly back and meet the team."

"Fly back? Where is back? I thought you were located here in San Diego," I said.

"No, we are located in Orlando, Florida. We interview out here in California because this is the Aerospace capital of the U.S. and is where all the experience that we need is located. We don't have much of a talent pool in Orlando. Orlando is a great city, growing, and it is a great place to raise kids in. However, it is short on Aerospace personnel"

On the way home, I had two hours to think about how I was going to tell Renee that I have an interview in Orlando. I think now about how fortunate we were to not have cell phones. If I did, I'm sure Renee would have been on the cell, calling me, way before I got home, asking about the interview. As it was, the two-hour drive was going fast enough, it just seemed my drive home was much faster than going. I pulled into our driveway, sat there a couple of minutes, I took a slow walk to the door, and I opened it. There was Renee, smiling with anticipation.

"How did the interview go? Do you have a second interview? Where in San Diego is the company located?" Renee asked.

"The interview went well. Yes, I have been asked to go back for a second interview. And, well, the company isn't located in San Diego," I said.

"Not in San Diego? Then where is it located? Is it closer to L.A.?"

"No. It is located in Orlando, Florida."

"ORLANDO!??? I'm not moving to Orlando. There is no way that we are moving to Orlando, period."

With that Renee walked away.

A week later, I landed in Orlando, got a rental car, found my way to the Red Roof Inn, and prepared for my interview the next day. The next morning, I had a continental breakfast consisting of a bowl of cereal and a banana that cost me five dollars (and this was in 1984). I had three interviews that morning and one in the afternoon. My flight home was at 4:30 PM. The morning sessions went well, I was asked to stay after lunch to meet, Gary, the VP of Finance. All my interviews were in the tower, a seven-story structure, and were with Directors of various positions. I was getting the heavy hand. That afternoon, I meet Gary in his office and he didn't waste anytime to start drilling me on my experience and know-how. I believe I was doing well responding to his questions, it just wasn't very much fun.

This continued for about 20 minutes until I remembered that, in one of my interviews earlier that day, someone said that Gary came from Ford Motors in Salinas, California. While at Hughes, I traveled to Ford Motors, in Salinas, to lead a negotiation team. In between one of the questions, I made the comment about his coming from Ford and that I had been at that facility. The change was dramatic. He pulled a low-level coffee table closer to him, kicked up his feet, put his hands behind his head and began talking about his experience at Ford Motors. He talked for the rest of the interview, so much so, that I began to get concerned about making my flight.

At one of his pauses, I said, "Just want to let you know I have a flight at 4:30."

Gary looked at his watch, it was about 3:15 PM, "Oh, you have a few more minutes yet."

With that, he continued his talking. I am not sure when the interview was finished, what I do know is that I was on the plane for two minutes when they shut the door.

A few weeks later I received a phone call.

"Hello may I speak to Mel King?"

"This is Mel."

"Hi Mel, my name is John and I am the HR Director here at Martin Marietta. Do you have a few minutes?"

"Sure," I said.

"Mel, your interviews went very well with all the Directors and the VP of Finance here at Martin; and, I have a request to bring back for a couple more interviews. In addition, we would like for you to bring your wife with you."

"Well, how soon are you talking about us coming there?"

"We would like for you to come Monday of the following week."

"Humm, that won't be possible. We have a trip planned for London beginning the Saturday prior to that Monday. We fly from L.A. to Boston and then over to London."

"What time is your flight out of Boston?"

"It is late afternoon early evening."

"Tell you what, what if I can arrange for the interviews to take place the Friday before. You arrive here on Thursday, interview on Friday, and we'll pay for the plane ticket to catch your original flight in Boston on Saturday."

Renee was pregnant with Darien, our third child at the time. All we would have to do, to make this thing happen with Martin Marietta is to leave a day earlier.

We arrived in Orlando, picked up a rental car, and headed to the hotel where John told us where we were staying. We walk into the hotel and I am immediately impressed. This was no Red Roof Inn. Really nice lobby. We walk into the elevator, has a waterfall on the outside. We come out of the chute and look out over an atrium. This is no Red Roof Inn.

The bell hop takes us to our room opens the door, a suite, sweet. This in no Red Roof Inn. The next morning, I go down for breakfast. A chef takes my order, for an omelet, I get hash browns, pancakes, OJ and bacon, no cost. Remember at Red Roof Inn, I paid $5.00 for a bowl of cereal and a banana. I thought, MMC was not doing this to impress me, it was Renee that they had in mind. I finished breakfast and went to MMC for a couple more interviews. At noon, the HR manager came by and picked Renee and I up from the hotel. We drove toward the Disney World property to the Grand Marquis, a five-star hotel, for lunch. We walked into the hotel and passed an eight-foot-long Chinese Junk that was made out of Jade. Wow! We hadn't seen anything like that except when we were in Japan and saw a grand piano made out of marble. Very impressive. In the restaurant, we were seated at a reserved table that looked out over the three, connecting swimming pools. The ambiance was fabulous. That meal, when we completed it, was $125. And remember, this was in 1984. John told us that he had reservations for last night, at this same restaurant, but since Renee wasn't feeling well, he opted to bring us here for lunch instead. Boy, was MMC going all out to please Renee.

That afternoon, we were lined up with a real estate broker that would take us to various parts of the city to show us housing, schools and provide info and answers to questions we may have about where to live.

We were surprised when he asked, "What size acre lot would you like? Half acre, three quarters or full acre lot?"

We were floored. In LA, a quarter acre lot was big. I had no idea how big a half acre lot was. A full acre sounded like a farm to us. Later that evening two of the Finance Directors and their wives took us to dinner at an Italian restaurant. As we approached the front door of the restaurant, the Maître 'D came out of the restaurant and opened the door.

"Good evening, Mr. Barnes. We have a table waiting for you and your guests. Please follow me." The Maître 'D said.

Impressive.

We walked inside and was immediately escorted to a reserved table. A waiter stood next to the table the whole time. Several times during the evening, I would reach for the pepper or salt, whoosh, the waiter would be there, grab the salt and present it, yes present it to me. Impressive. Every time I reached for something, whoosh. The guy was good. The evening was very relaxing and it wasn't until the end of the dinner that one of the directors broached the subject of hiring.

"Mel, you made quite an impression with all who interviewed you. Martin is interested in hiring you but we wouldn't be able to do anything until after the first of the year. Would that be a problem with you?"

"No, the delay would not be a problem. But I want you to know, I am doing very well at Hughes and I am well respected in the company," I said.

I did not comment about my feelings of unequal treatment or recognition, but the 'respect' I did believe is true.

"That is not surprising to us. We believe we can make it worth your while to make the move and join our team. When that time comes, John, the HR manager will have all the details."

. This was in November of 1984. The next morning Renee and I caught our flight to Boston to start our vacation in London.

London

Our vacation was planned so that we would spend four days in London and three days in Paris. We were having a great time in London and so expressed that to a taxi driver.

"You know, we have really enjoyed it here in London, we plan to go to Paris next to complete our holiday," I told the cab driver.

The British use the word "holiday" for vacation.

The driver said, "Why would you want to go to Paris? Do you speak French? You won't have as much fun if you don't. In fact, they can be rather rude, the bloody chaps. Tell you what, will you stay in London if I get you tickets to a play that has been sold out for months? There is an 8:00 PM performance tonight. Give me a couple of hours and I will have them at the ticket booth at Will Call."

"OK, deal. You get the tickets and we'll stay in London. There is a lot more we want to see anyway."

There is so much to say about London and our experience in the countryside. The cabbie came through with the tickets, and, wow! Did he come through. Orchestra center seating about six rows from the stage. Since he kept his side of the bargain, we kept ours and stayed in England for the remainder of our Holiday. We enjoyed the time so much we didn't regret going to Paris.

On one of our field trips, Renee and I took a picture with one of the Palace Guards. After we had our photo taken a lady came up to take our place and stood next to the guard. All the guards are trained to be very stoic, rigid and non-responsive to the environment. They don't smile, scratch, or interact in anyway with what is happening around them. They do move but only at appointed times. When this lady came and stood next to the guard, it so happened that it was at that moment the guard lifts up his gargantuan shoes, does a quarter turn and stomps down. When his foot hit the ground, it could be heard a block away. The lady hollered and almost fainted, for two reasons. One the guard moved, secondly, when the guard brought his foot down it made a very loud noise. Oh yeah, a third. When his foot went down it landed almost on top of hers. I bet she felt the vibration as it hit the ground. All of us watching began laughing. All in all, it was just so unexpected. We looked at the guard and saw a twinkle in his eye and a slight quiver around the lips. He knew what he had done. Obviously, this lady's reaction was customary and was the one area that broke the guard's routine. Prior to this we wondered if the guards were even human, afterwards, we left with a better appreciation of their human side.

We, in the U.S. think a structure that was built in the 1800's is old. Well, we saw the house that Shakespeare was born in, with people still living in it. And then we went to Windsor castle, the place where Joan of Arc was tried, and is a residence of the British royal family. Then we went to Strafford upon Avon, to see Ann Hathaway's house, the wife of Shakespeare. Along the way, on many of our tours, we always stopped for "a spot of tea." The British are big on their teas and biscuits or I should say, a variety of biscuits. In fact, they don't have breakfast as we do in the U.S. Their breakfast is this selection of teas and their biscuits, either plain or filled with all sorts of preserves. This was novel the first four days, by the fifth day, all I wanted was some good 'ole bacon, eggs and hash-browns.

Leaving Hughes

It was in March of 1985 that I gave my two weeks' notice to Hughes. I can't say that the company made countless counter offers, it didn't happen. I do know, on the day that I checked out, the HR manager, who was fairly new and of which I had little contact, wanted an exit interview with me. He admitted to being dumbfounded as to why the company was letting me go without a fight. He saw that, even after seven years, I was one of only three Black managers at the division. As far as he was concern, this was a slap in the face of affirmative action. Moreover, he said that since he didn't know me, he asked several people about me who did. He said their response piqued his curiosity. He began to ask others about me as well. The picture that he began to form, he said, was amazing and totally baffling.

"There was not one negative comment, all spoke very highly of you and often supported their position with things that you had done for them and the company. With you being Black, with this kind of record, Black or White, there is no way the company should be letting you go. This is one instance where truly, this is our loss. I don't understand it, but I wish you well."

Once again, I thought about General Olds. "Civilians don't often appreciate nor reward leadership, innovation, or dedication. The service does and has recognized innate leadership in you; which, will not necessarily be so in the civilian sector where politics and envy can come into play."

If I were not Black, would the outcome have been different? I suspect so. Why? Unbeknownst to the Controller, I was aware that one of my peers received an out of cycle raise. He had not done anything close to contributing to the company in a manner that I had done. It just so happened that the two of them were really good friends. For the many things I did, the money that I saved and earned for the company, you would think that the company would have shown its appreciation. Nada, once again. Being Black, being of a different culture, or not being considered "one of the boys," had its disadvantages. However, I considered my work would be for the long-term compensation, as in working for the Lord. It is tough though. The flesh wants to be rewarded now.

Accomplishments at the Traveling Wave Tube Division:

- Within months, restored Estimating & Pricing to a functional and valued department
- Became the lead spokesperson for the Division when explaining what we do to non-engineering clients and visitors
- Became the lead negotiator for the Division, even though I was not in the Contracts organization
  - o Successfully negotiated every contract in which I was appointed
  - o Minimized/ reduced the number of personnel required for negotiations
  - o Increased profit margins significantly
  - o All programs of which I negotiated made a profit
- Became the primary contact point for any DCAA (Defense Contract Audit Agency) issues or inquiries (This agency could stop our organization from doing business with the Government if issues were not resolved or rectified in a satisfactory manner)
- Successfully gained financial cooperation from a Research & Development department where three other Managers from Finance failed
- Pioneered department level Finance Manager position

- Purchased first desktop PC at Hughes Aircraft
- Utilized PC to standardize Estimating process with resultant efficiency in time and accuracy
- Developed "Early Warning" report that identified monthly over/under profit position of Division contracts, held by each department. Assistant Controller began using report to extract excess profit from programs where profits were previously hidden by department Business Managers.
- Oversight responsibility for major estimates, such as: AAMRAM, F-14 TWT, F-18 TWT and others
- One of only three Black Managers in a Division of 3500 personnel
- Obtained my MBA degree, graduating with 3.7 G.P.A.

Since I was not a political person, it is unfortunate that the many accomplishments that were made for the company were neither formally recognized nor rewarded in a monetary sense. Yet I witnessed those that could not claim similar accomplishments/ achievements be rewarded monetarily.

Leaving Los Angeles

Members of the "Crew" (CCC TV Crew) and other friends gave Renee and I a going-away party that also included a "This is your Life" episode. It was a lot of fun and something that every person should have happen once in their life. Just before we left town, Renee and I had our annual anniversary dinner with Vic & George, Ron & Josie, and Mike & Bev. The three couples, excluding my sister and her husband all got married in April, 1978, on subsequent weekends.

Every year, the last weekend in April we would get together and all go out to dinner. Vic & George tagged along just as an excuse to get out of the house. This last meeting before we would leave town was our seventh dinner together. At the dinner, we made an agreement that we would go on a cruise for our 10th anniversary.

I left to go to Florida in April, 1985. Renee stayed in L. A. for about six months before joining me in Orlando. Renee's dad, Al, went with me on the initial trip to help drive my car back to Orlando. It took us 64 hours (This time would become meaningful when compared to a later trip).

Couldn't end this chapter without showing Renee in her "Do" for her graduation picture at West L.A. Junior College.

Mr. King has written several short stories of his life as a young boy and teenager. One such story is contained here as a Bonus entry.

Bridgeport (cornfields)

It was a puffy cloud day, and the hum of a small engine plane sounded like a honey bee when it darts from flower to flower gathering pollen. We lay in the down softness of the summer grass and had tired of identifying faces in the clouds, so we set off to see what adventure the woods would have for us that day. We lived in the country about six miles from the city airport. At night, the beacon atop the control tower pierced the darkness for miles. During the day, you could never tell there was an airport around except for the occasional humming as a plane came in on its final approach.

From our low vantage point, we could only see the corn and soybean fields that seemed to cover the whole earth. Now, most grown-ups would look at those fields and just see corn and soybean. The more observant grown up would see the lustrous gold of the soybean and verdant green of the corn. Others would pass and not give the fields a second notice. But to us, these fields were the fields of dreams . . .

Ah yes, even now I can see Billy. He was the oldest of us guys, tall and lanky. His parents had chickens, a pig yard, and corn and soybean fields. I was no more than nine or 10 years old, but some mornings, I would wake up at 4:30 AM, get dressed, and walk the half mile by myself to his house to help Billy feed the chickens and slop the hogs. He was an only child, so he really appreciated my help. I would do this in the dark, three or four times a week during spring, summer, or autumn. After we finished with the hogs, we would check the hen house for any freshly laid eggs and bring them into the main house for breakfast. His parents fixed two kinds of meat, eggs, potatoes, biscuits, gravy, and plenty of milk. But before we could eat, we had to stack the feed corn and make sure the sows had plenty to eat and drink and the piglets made it through the night (pigs can be cannibalistic). We were plenty hungry by the time we sat down to eat.

I made the trek to Billy's house at such early hours and helped him with his chores because my family couldn't always afford to have breakfast as I had breakfast at Billy's house. I was the sixth of eight children, my mom was a stay-at-home mom, and my dad, as a cabinet maker and house builder in and around Indianapolis, didn't always have a contract in which to work; but somehow managed to have provisions for our family, though we were on the poor side of the economic scale. Fortunately, I didn't know we were poor. We always had something to eat, even if it was beans and rice, and we always had clean clothes to wear. Anyhow, we had to finish the chores, eat breakfast, and get out to the mailbox by 7:10 AM so the school bus could pick us up; otherwise, we had a long walk/run to school, about four miles by road and two as the crow flies or through the corn fields. Sometimes, Billy would act all crazy and stuff, like refuse to do his chores or purposely miss the school bus. When he did, I usually did not go to his house and help him with his chores. Besides, he would almost always be on a couple days' punishment. I would stay home and catch the bus from our house.

At the corner of our property and at a "T" intersection sat this huge tree in which my older brothers built a tree house. Since my dad was a carpenter and house builder, my older brothers had access to tools and materials that made them the envy of their age group. This access was the key to the design and manner in which our tree house was built, which was no ordinary tree house. This was a split-level tree house, meaning it had three rooms at different levels within the tree, all connected. It was enclosed with windows designated "scrap" from a job my dad had done in remodeling a house. It didn't stop there; this tree house even had a door. To cap it off, there was an outside deck to sit on where we could take advantage of the height and see in every direction. From this vantage point, we could see for miles the soybean and corn fields waving in a soft breeze, waving as if they were beckoning us to come and explore. We could even see more clearly the regional airport and the small planes, buzzing like honey bees, taking off, and landing. It is amazing to see how this quaint little regional airport has since transformed to the much larger and busier Indianapolis International Airport.

We accessed the tree house by climbing a thick rope with knots tied about every foot. Often, we would also swing with the rope, and the county helped us do so. Ever-so-often, the country trimmed the tree's branches to make sure they did not interfere or get tangled with school buses or farm equipment passing under it. This trimming created a nice open space for swinging. The rope was tied very high up in the tree to maximize the swing and take advantage of the branch cutting. Sometimes, though, the rope would come undone from where we had secured it. When it did, the rope would make a loop, hang like a loose snake above the road in the middle of the intersection, and interfere with the school bus's passage. When this happened, the bus driver would yell out to any family member, "King," and any one of us Kings would get off the bus, scamper up the tree, secure the rope, and get back on the bus. Everybody on the bus thought this was way cool.

John lived back up Hoffman Road about a half mile. He was older than me, younger than Billy, and real strong. I think he got his strength from hauling pigs around all day. John's parents also had chickens, a pig yard, and corn and soybean fields. We all liked one thing about John's dad. He would go to one of the huge bakeries in town, pick up all their "day-old" bread, and bring it back to the pigs to mix it in their gruel. What we liked were the cakes, cookies, and other pastries that often came back with him. Mind you, this was not a pick-up truck, but a truck the size of a dump truck. Sometimes our tree house would be so full of cookies and donuts we would use them for ammunition in our mock war games.

And then there was Steve. Steve lived in Nap town aka Indianapolis and was like a cousin. He was a little awkward, a little clumsy, but a lot of fun to be around. He took it good naturedly when we teased him about being a "city boy." During the summer, he spent a lot of time at our house, so he joined us on a lot of adventures. This was one of his first.

Throughout the summer, we had gone on many a safari, treasure hunt, and journeys to faraway places within the corn and soybean fields. On one such journey, we organized a safari hunt to seek and capture big game. We knew the risk. The hunter can easily become the hunted. Before we set off on our quest, we took stock of our weapons and ammunition: We all carried slingshots, two tree branches roughly the shape of a rifle, and our prized possession, a Red Flyer BB gun. It had seen a few years; the stock was real wood, cracked but expertly taped and worn smooth from use. The working mechanism was well oiled and had maintained its compression over the years.

BBs were scarce, and we rarely used them. But on a safari, one could never tell what to expect, so we gathered what few BBs we could find and made John, the ammo bearer, hand over his prized marble for collateral. As the transfer was made, the marble caught the sun, and a brilliant radiance emanated from John's marble. We all gasped at the unexpected sight. No wonder John picked this marble as his most valued.

I safely tucked it away in a pocket that buttoned. In our pockets, we each had a few rocks, candy and a cookie for our rations, and marbles for when we set up camp—after all, we had to bring some sort of entertainment. It was time to go. Well, we saw enough John Wayne and Tarzan movies to know when to march in a straight line or side by side. That day, because of the cornfield and the peril we imagined would be lurking within, we walked in a straight line, one person behind the other.

We walked the fringe of the jungle to get our bearings and try to discover if any trees in the nearby forest would be a good landmark. We always established a rallying point in case we got separated, a place to mend the wounded or bury the dead. Well, we saw our tree, and from that point, we turned and headed deeper into the jungle. The corn, extraordinarily tall this year, towered over us and shut out the noise of the world. We were on our own.

As we walked, Billy almost stepped on a rabbit's burrow. This was not uncommon; what was uncommon was the long-eared rabbit that jumped out. We all screamed, hollered, and didn't know which way to run. When we recovered, fortunately our pants were still dry, three slingshots and a BB gun took aim. We marveled at the shots we had taken and the number of hits. One corn stalk had its ear of corn hanging by a thread, and several other stalks had good-sized holes in their leaves. The rabbit, with twitching whiskers and big black eyes, had been in more danger of knocking itself out on a corn stalk in its haste than from us hitting it with a rock or BB. As the rabbit hopped away and out of danger (if ever it was in danger from us), we laughed and chuckled at ourselves. We prided ourselves as expert marksmen with the slingshot and BB gun . . . couldn't tell that this day.

As we told the rabbit story for about the tenth time, something felt different . . . strange. It was a sixth sense. Something told us we were in danger: we were being hunted. Trouble was, we didn't know the direction or source of the danger. We just knew something was wrong. As we stood looking into the eyes of one another, curiosity on our faces, slightly, oh so slightly, we felt a slight tremor in the ground beneath our feet. Finally, we heard the unmistakable rumble of corn thrashing machines. These were the elephants of our jungle; they ruled, and they were stampeding. We were about to violate one of the basic laws of our jungle: don't run across the rows of corn, but travel between them. The leaves look limp and harmless, but herein lies the danger, taking the leaves for granted and not respecting them. When you move fast, and we were moving fast, these leaves are like thousands of razor blades seeking exposed skin to cut. The jungle is like that, you know. Danger lurks in the most unexpected places. If you are not careful, you can get cut up pretty bad just by walking through the corn, and running makes it worse.

But when the elephants stampede, quicksand and lions are not a concern, and neither were the cuts and bruises we knew we were getting. Come on, feet, help the body; we got a crisis here! We could hear the elephants getting closer and the ground rumbling louder. It would be close. We had just cleared a row of corn when one elephant went by. These elephants were huge monsters, at least 12 feet high and 15 feet wide. The only way to deal with these babies was to run. Fortunately, the elephants run in what is called a "chorus line." One elephant follows the other in a staggered manner with a little overlap to assure total coverage of the field. Well, we knew the next one was coming. What we didn't know was how many, how fast, and how far one was behind the other. We ran for an eternity. And, just as we cleared one row of corn, the next elephant passed by. We were losing ground. As we ran through the corn, our bodies bled from the multiple cuts we received. This was truly becoming a "rite of passage."

Another elephant passed and nicked Steve's shoe. Steve went down, arms and legs sprawled every which way. We stopped, went back to pick Steve up, and ran off again. Now we knew we would never cross the path in time to get clear of the next elephant. We ran, knowing we were in trouble as we waited for the inevitable. Steve began crying, John shouted, and Billy and I encouraged them both to run faster. The final elephant bore down on us. Its roar sounded loudest, and the ground shook and rumbled the most than it ever had. We saw flashbacks of our past, which went fairly quickly since we were not that old. Although fear had energized us to run faster, in the end it also paralyzed us. We waited for the inevitable. Even though the ground rumbling and the general noise of the elephants passing became even louder, we heard the instrument of our passing, the whir of the combine blades. We closed our eyes and waited. Suddenly, we heard three loud blasts. With those three blasts, it got very quiet and still, the air itself didn't move, and I thought, Wow, it sure is quiet in Heaven. Will eternity be this quiet? Then we heard a door slam. I peeked with one eye to see if I could recognize where I was or see any of the angels around me . . . and I thought, Strange, that angel looks just like Mr. Peters. Then the angel spoke, and it was Mr. Peters. Mr. Peters looked like how you would expect a farmer to look. He wore jean coveralls with a matching cap and had a twinkle in his eyes and a ready grin on his face.

"What in the dickens are you boys doing here?"

We all talked at once, except Steve. Steve was still in shock and recuperating from our recent episode. Finally, Mr. Peters quieted us down and asked Billy to talk to him. Mr. Peters listened to Billy talk, which was strange for Mr. Peters, since he was known to give orders, and rarely did anyone ever talk "to" him. Billy told him how we were tracking big game and found the rabbit. The telling evolved into a story about the biggest rabbit this side of the Mississippi, which came out of its burrow to attack us, and how we wounded this gigantic rabbit multiple of times. When Billy stopped talking, Mr. Peters looked at us and got this big ole smile on his face. "Well, I reckon the angels were working overtime today. The only reason we stopped the chorus line was because something happened to the lead machine." Mr. Peters said. Fortunately for us, each machine following the lead machine had to stop. They had no idea we were in their path. The three horn blasts we heard was a signal to let the drivers know that a machine had stopped and all other machines were to stop.

"Lord only knows what would have happened if something didn't stop the lead machine," Mr. Peters said. Well, we told Mr. Peters we would leave the jungle now, but had one favor to ask.

"Well what favor can I do you boys?" asked Mr. Peters.

"Well, Mr. Peters, in our running, we don't know which direction or how far we ran. What we need to do is to get our bearings so we will know how to get out of this jungle, uh, cornfield and head home. Would you mind if we climbed up on the side of your elephant, uh, combine so we can get our bearings?"

"No, but just have one of you boys go up. Don't want to keep those angels busier than they need to be."

Billy, the oldest and tallest, volunteered to climb the side of the elephant and see if he could locate the tree we had designated as our land mark. It didn't take long before he yelled down to us, "I see it. I know which way we need to go." Once Billy rejoined us on the ground, we thanked Mr. Peters for stopping the stampede.

"Come on, Steve. Let's go," I said.

"'Come on, Steve. Let's go.'" Steve said. "Do you guys realize what just happened here? We could have been killed, and all you say is, 'Come on, Steve. Let's go.' I'm gonna go, al' right, I'm gonna go back home . . . to the city. You guys are crazy."

Billy, John, and I laughed so hard even Mr. Peters smiled. We put our arms around Steve and said, "You ain't seen nothing yet. That was just your first safari."

We turned to Mr. Peters, thanked him again for stopping the elephants, and then set off toward our rendezvous point, and from there, home.

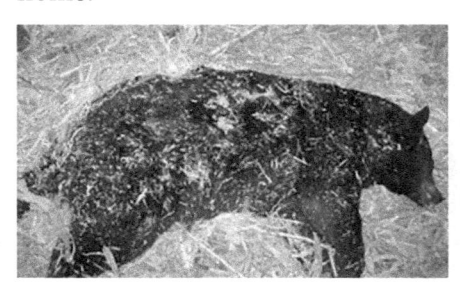

This bear, which weighed nearly 400 pounds when alive, was killed by a corn combine on Saturday, Nov. 6, 2010, about eight miles southeast of Red Wing. (Courtesy to Pioneer Press: Tyler Quandt, Minnesota)